Apostolic Ministerial Manual

EDITOR-IN-CHIEF

Eric A. Beda, MBA

Published in the United States by
Alpha Omega Publishing Company
P.O. Box 353, Jackson, MI 49204
Library of Congress Control Number: 2017962179

ISBN: 978-1-7320586-9-9

All Scripture quotations are derived from the Holy Bible, King James Version and the New King James Version.

Alpha Omega Publishing Company publishes books that promote the discussion and understanding of the Pentecostal movement throughout the world since the day of Pentecost. These books are made possible by the enthusiasm of our readers; the support of a committed group of donors, large and small; the collaboration of our many partners in the independent media and ecclesiastical organizations; booksellers, who often hand-sell Alpha Omega Publishing books; librarians; and above all by our authors.
Books may be purchased in quantity and/or special sales by contacting the publisher:

Alpha Omega Publishing
517-879-1286
E: info@omegapublishing.org
www.omegapublishing.org

Printed in the United States of America

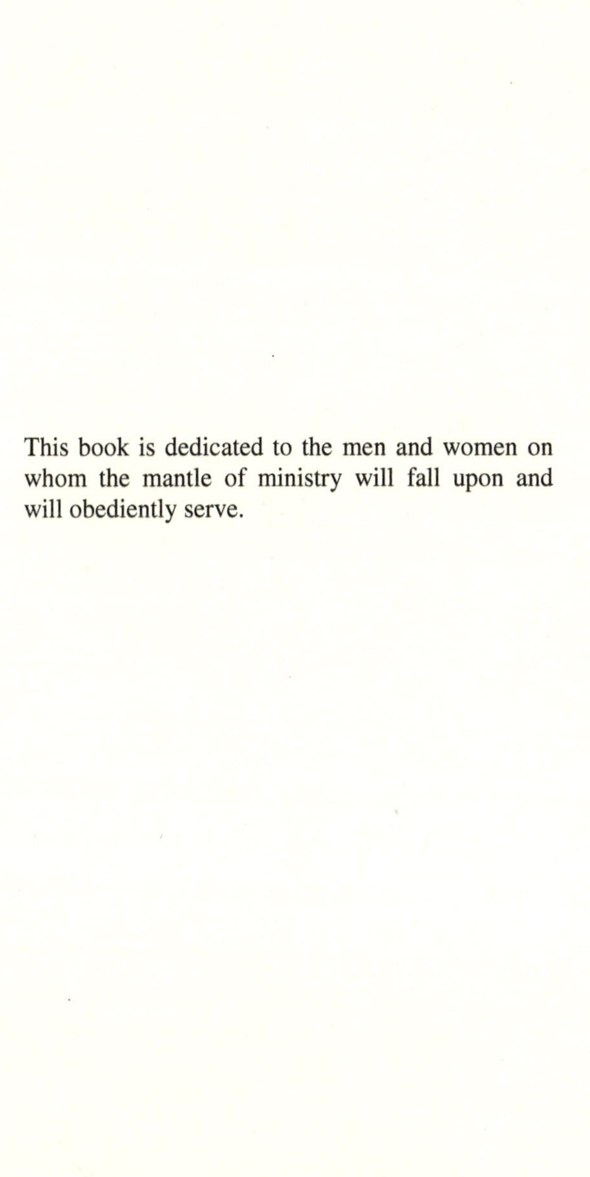

This book is dedicated to the men and women on whom the mantle of ministry will fall upon and will obediently serve.

Table of Content

FOREWORD

It is my religious duty and privilege to recommend this manual that contains a small part of the doctrines and disciplines of the Apostolic faith. This book is meant to serve as an instrument in a preacher's toolbox.

I have read many books in my lifetime, including the Holy Bible more than forty times and I find this manual to be an absolute must-have for Apostolic preachers. We need more materials in our toolbox and less philosophical books in our libraries.

I was born in Portsmouth, Ohio, April 1, 1930, which was a transitional period for many Pentecostal groups. Growing up my father, John Andrew James was known as a serious person, an analytical thinker, and a devout Methodist pastor. But change came into our home when my mother, Bertha James, received the Gospel, and was baptized in the name of Jesus and filled with the precious Holy Ghost in 1931. I often say, my first birth made me a citizen of the United States of America, and the second birth provided me citizenship in heaven.

I am Apostolic from the crown of my head to the sole of my feet. I am Pentecostal in experience and Apostolic in doctrine. The Gospel is the world's most significant message, and the Apostolic doctrine is the world's best method by which the gospel is bestowed upon man. This book offers the Apostolic minister especially, those new to the ministry tools by which they can perform sacred ceremonies within the context of the Apostolic doctrine.

Elder Johnny James
"The Walking Bible"

INTRODUCTION

The first edition of the Pentecostal Ministerial Manual is reflective of the creed and doctrinal position of the Pentecostal Assemblies of the World, the United Pentecostal Church International, Pentecostal Churches of the Apostolic Faith International, Apostolic World Christian Fellowship, and other Pentecostal Apostolic organizations with like precious faith. Although the word of God is the only sufficient rule of faith and practices, the church, in the liberty given to it by the Lord, is fully authorized to make these scriptural suggestions.

Thomas Jefferson once described the presidency as "a splendid misery." I don't believe it's an appropriate narrative of the ministry while others may argue otherwise. It is the highest calling on the face of the earth ,and there is no other calling that is of similar value in the sight of God. There is no calling that is more rewarding, and at the same time, more demanding than being a minister. The modern minister faces a multitude of tasks that are both electrifying and challenging. He must conduct funerals and weddings, often on the same day. He must be a shepherd, a scholar, a public speaker, an educator, a financier, a CEO, a personnel manager, a counselor, and at times a family man.

While it's true Christians are facing challenges for the sake of the gospel, apostolic ministers are facing more opposition for their stance on the one Lord, one faith, and one baptism message in the name of Jesus Christ.

The apostolic church is a continuation of the great revival that began at Jerusalem on the day of Pentecost, 30 A.D. (Acts 2:1-12). It is *built on the foundation of the apostles and prophets, Jesus Christ himself being the chief cornerstone* (Ephesians 2:19-20). All Christ faithful followers have been little known, yet from that time until now, there have been earnest contenders for the faith that was once delivered unto the saints (Jude 1:3).

The Pentecostal Ministerial Manual was developed with a new apostolic minister in mind. The purpose of this manual is to foster support and standardize certain practices among Apostolic churches globally. Let us labor together in the spirit of unity that we might fully secure the end for which the church was founded.

Eric A. Beda

Editor-In-Chief

Alpha Omega Publishing

ARTICLES OF RELIGION

Article 1: The Apostolic Doctrine and Fellowship

Our creed, discipline, rules of order, and doctrine is the Word of God as taught and revealed by the Holy Spirit (St. John 14:26, I Corinthians 2:9-13).

All scripture is given by the inspiration of God, and is profitable for doctrine, for reproof, for correction, for instruction in righteousness, that the man of God may be perfect, thoroughly furnished unto all good works (II Timothy 3:16-17).

As members of the Body of Christ, which is the true church (Ephesians 1:22-23), the Word of God declares but one way of entrance therein ,and that is *by one Spirit are we all baptized into one Body* and that is a baptism of *Water and Spirit* (I

Corinthians 12:12-27, Galatians 3:26-28, Romans 6:3-4, St. John 3:5, Acts 2:38).

Article 2: The Godhead

The Apostolic faith organizations believe in the mystery of the Godhead (Acts 17:29, Colossians 2:9). The Lord was pleased to manifest Himself as a father: the source of all life; as a son: the channel and redeemer of mankind; and as the Holy Ghost: the comforter, revealer, and inspiration of life.

The Father is the invisible God who is made manifest in the personification of the son named Jesus while the Holy Ghost is the invisible power of God working in the church. The Father is God in *creation (*Genesis 1:1; 2:7; Isaiah 40:28), the Son is God in *redemption* (Isaiah 9:6; 44:6; 44:24; 47:4; St. Luke 2:10-11; St. John 1:1; 1:10-14; 4:40-42; 10:30; Acts 20:28; Titus 2:10-13; I Timothy 1:1-3), and the Holy Spirit is God in *inspiration* (St. John 4:23-24) and *comfort* (St. John 14:26; 15:26; 16:7). When one manifestation of the Godhead is patent, the other two are latent (St. John 14:6-13). Jesus is both human and divine: He is both Creator and creature. He is the son of Mary and her God simultaneously. Further, He is God manifested in the flesh (I Timothy 3:16) ,and our Eternal Father made visible (Isaiah 9:6)—apart from whom, there is no God (Isaiah 43:10-11; St. John 8:24; Revelation 1:17; 22:13). According to Scripture, the one visible God will be our Lord Jesus Christ at the final consummation of all things.

Article 3: Name of God

The Apostolic church subscribes to the belief that God changed His name periodically to suit the dispensational needs of His people. His present dispensational name is the Lord Jesus Christ (St. John 20:25-28).

Article 4: Repentance and Remission of Sins

To whoever will accept God's way, an entrance into the everlasting kingdom of our Lord and savior Jesus Christ shall be offered abundantly (St. John 10:1-9). God will accept anyone into His kingdom that has a broken and contrite heart for wrongdoings (Psalms 51:17). John the Baptist preached repentance, and Jesus proclaimed repentance. He commanded His disciples to preach in His name among all nations, beginning at Jerusalem, the message of repentance and remission of sins (Luke 24:47). Peter was able to fulfill this command on the Day of Pentecost (Acts 2:38).

Article 5: Record of Membership

The names of the members of God's church are kept on record in Heaven (Luke 10:20). For it is written, *The Lord shall count, when He writeth up the people, that this man was born there* (Psalms 87:6). All must be "born of water and of the Spirit" (St. John 3:5) in this dispensation if one desires that their name is written in heaven or the book of life (Philippians 4:3). Additionally, it is imperative that each local church keeps a record of its membership.

Article 6: Second Birth

We believe the second birth to be limited to the human family only, and it is attained by being born of water and the spirit. (St. John 3:5). Subsequently, the resurrection is limited to the human family as well (Matthew 22:30; St. John 11:24; Romans 6:5; Revelation 20:6).

Article 7: How Names Are Blotted Out

Blotting names out is an action performed by God in His sovereignty; we have no input in this matter. *And the LORD said unto Moses, Whosoever hath sinned against me, him will I blot out of my book"* (Exodus 32:33). Likewise, *He that overcometh, the same shall be clothed in white raiment; and I will not blot out his name out of the book of life, but I will confess his name before my Father, and before his angels* (Revelation 3:5).

Article 8: God's Standard of Salvation

We must earnestly contend for the faith and God's standard of salvation. This standard is a Holy Spirit-filled life with signs and miracles such as on the day of Pentecost (I John 3:2-3; Mark 16:16-18; Acts 2:4; 8:14-17; 9:17-18; 10:44-48; 19:1-6; Romans 12:1-21; Hebrews 12:14; Matthew 5:48; I Peter 1:15-16).

Article 9: The Wholly Sanctified Life

To escape the judgement of God and to have the hope of enjoying the glory of life eternal, one must be thoroughly saved from their sins—wholly sanctified unto God and filled with the Holy Ghost (Hebrews 12:14, I Peter 1:15-17). A wholly sanctified life is the only real standard of a Christian life.

Article 10: The Lord's Supper

Melchizedek, the priest of the highest God, gave the first communion consisting of bread and wine to our father Abraham (Genesis 14:18-19). Christ as a *high priest for ever after the order of Melchizedek* (Hebrews 6:20) administered the same (Matthew 26:26-29; I Corinthians 11:23-26). Grape juice and water are modern substitutes for wine which have been introduced by the formal churches of today—in which many have never been regenerated and born of the Spirit (1 Corinthians 11:27-34).

Article 11: Foot Washing

Foot washing is a decree that Jesus made before his departure from his disciples. It is an ordinance just as any other New Testament commandment. Jesus instructed that we ought to wash one another's feet, but we can first learn from his example of how to perform the act as He did (St. John 13:14-17). There is also scriptural evidence that the church practiced this act in the days of the Apostle Paul (I Timothy 5:10).

Article 12: Healing by Faith

The Lord is our healer; Jesus is the great physician (Exodus 15:26; Psalms 103:2-3; Matthew 8:14-17; Isaiah 53:4-5; Mark 16:17-18; James 5:14-16). *With his stripes we are healed* (Isaiah 53:5). Should it be thought inconceivable that the Lord should be able to heal the bodies He made?

Article 13: The Return of Jesus

A doctrine clearly outlined in apostolic times is that Jesus is coming back in person. Jesus taught it, the Apostles preached it, and the saints expected it. The following is only a portion of the scriptural references on the subject: I Thessalonians 4:16-17; Titus 2:12-14; Matthew 24:30-31, 36-39; 25:31; Revelation 1:7.

Article 14: Translation of the Saints

We believe that the time is drawing near for the return of the Lord where he will make a change in the present dispensation of time. During the coming of Jesus, all those that have already died in righteousness shall arise from their graves while those who are living righteously before God shall be translated to meet the Lord in the air (I Thessalonians 4:16-17). The following is only a segment of the scriptural references on the subject: Matthew 24:36-42; Luke 17:20-37; I Corinthians 15:51-54; Philippians 3:20-21; I Thessalonians 5:1-10.

Article 15: The Millennium

The distress upon the earth is the beginning of sorrows and will become more intense (Matthew 24:3-12; Daniel 12:1-2); *there shall be a time of trouble, such as never was since there was a nation even to that same time* (Daniel 12:1). That period of tribulation will be followed by the dawn of a better day on earth, and for one thousand years thereafter, there shall be peace on earth and good will toward men (Luke 2:14). The scriptural references are: Matthew 5:5; Isaiah 65:17-25; Romans 11:26-27; Revelations 20:1-5.

Article 16: Final Judgment

When the thousand years have passed, there shall be a resurrection of the dead during which they shall be summoned before the great white throne for their final judgement. All whose names are not found written in the book of life shall be cast into the lake of fire, burning with brimstone, which God has prepared for the devil and his angels (Revelation 20:10). The following scriptures represent a portion of the theological references on the subject: Matthew 7:21-23; 25:31-46; Revelation 19:11-15; 20:10-15; 21:8.

Article 17: Relationship to Civil Government

God has ordained all civil ordinances for the peace, safety, and welfare of all people (Romans 13:1-14). Therefore, it is our duty to conform to all requirements of the law that are not contrary to the word of God or do not force us to the violation of the sixth commandment by bearing arms and taking life. We must honor our rulers, respect them in all requirements of the civil law, and, without murmuring, pay tribute as required (Matthew 17:24-27; 22:17-21).

Article 18: Maltreatment

The saints are encouraged, *if it be possible, as much as lieth in you, live peaceably with all men* (Romans 12:18). In times of persecution or ill-treatment at the hands of an enemy, one should not avenge themselves. As rehearsed by the Apostle Paul, *avenge not yourselves, but rather give place unto wrath: for it is written, Vengeance is mine; I will repay, saith the Lord* (Romans 12:19). Further, one should not take up any weapon to slay another, whether in self-defense or in defense of others. As it is written, *do violence to no man* (Luke 3:14). Jesus repeatedly preaches a message of peace instead of violence, no matter the circumstance (Matthew 26:52; St. John 18:10-11, 36). One should rather suffer wrong than do wrong.

Article 19: Secret Societies

According to the word of God, we firmly believe and hold that the people of God should have no connection with secret societies or any other organization or body wherein there is a fellowship of unbelievers bound by an oath (James 4:4). Members of God's church should not work as pickets or by any other measure bar others from their work. However, this does not abridge their rights to pay dues to the union and work for their families.

Article 20: Miscellaneous Rulers

Interracial relationships

We declare that we are mindful of the great evil of discrimination that is contrary to the Word of God and inconsistent with Christian practices. We, therefore, admonish all of our brethren to keep themselves pure from this evil and to seek its extinction by all lawful and Christian means. We must, at all times and in all places, welcome all groups into our midst as equal without regard to race, class, or any other unscriptural distinction (Hebrews 13:2, Acts 10:34-35).

Woman's Dress

Apostolic women should dress with modesty as becoming of saints. Rouge, lipstick, eye makeup, and nail polish should not be used to the extreme to decorate the physical body. Likewise, extreme, strange, or peculiar styles such as short dresses, low cut necks, or outlandish hairstyles are not encouraged (1 Timothy 2:9-10).

Recreation

We believe that the social instinct is God-given, and, if properly guided, it will strengthen rather than harm the spiritual life. However, we admonish you to be wise with recreational activities and set no injurious example in this matter. We adjure you to remember, the question for a Christian must not be whether a course of action is positively immoral, but whether it will dull the spiritual life and cause Christ to be evil spoken of (1 Timothy 4:8).

Marriage

Conforming to the Apostolic perception, our people be conformed to the spirit of not being unequally yoked with unbelievers. Our ministers should discourage saints from marrying persons other than believers. Many marriages between saints and unbelievers have had disastrous consequences; in some cases, the believer was hindered from a consecrated life or even turned back to the world entirely (II Corinthians 6:14).

Generally speaking, an under aged woman should not contract a marriage without the consent of her parents: yet there may be exceptions to this rule if a woman believes it to be her duty to get married, or if her parents absolutely refuse to let her marry a Christian. Then she may—if she is of age, marry without their consent.

Divorcement

No matter what a person's matrimonial ventures might have been before they came to the Lord, the church can only judge the individual from the time they came into the body of Christ. If they came in with marital entanglements—previous plural marriages without divorces or other forms of illegal marriages— it is the pastor's or church's duty to assist them in organizing their affairs.

Thereafter, if an unbelieving mate departs and legally severs the marriage bond, the believer is free to marry again.

There shall be no divorce and remarriage where both partners have been baptized of the Holy Ghost, except for the cause of fornication. The guilty party, whose fornication has resulted in the divorcement shall not be permitted to remarry while the innocent companion still lives. Should the guilty party marry one who does not know the status of their guilt, the ignorant party shall still be received into fellowship. Any further disposition of the cause should be to the discretion of the pastor of the church who shall have sole jurisdiction in the matter (1 Corinthians 7:1-17).

Article 21: Offering

The acts of begging, rallying, or shows in order to finance the work of the Lord are not according to God's plan. We believe that if the people of God would obey His word, there would be plenty on hand without anyone having to resort to scheming, grafting, or any other unholy method of raising money. Tithing and free will offering are God's plan (Genesis 14:20; 28:22; Malachi 3:8-12; Exodus 25:2; 35:5).

Solicitation of money on the streets—whether at random or during service— is not pleasing to the Lord. The impression is given that the people of God are more interested in money than in the salvation of the lost. This causes many to pass by who otherwise might stop to hear the gospel. We should preach the gospel without charge (1 Corinthians 9:18). If anyone feels disposed to give an offering, let it be gratefully received as from the Lord.

ORDER OF CEREMONIES

BAPTISM

Importance Of Baptism

Magnifying the Ordinances

As pastor and leader of worship, one must realize that the manner in which the baptism ceremony is observed is essential. Since our Lord left this ordinance to the church as a means of making sure the gospel message would be perpetuated, every time the church observes the ordinance in the proper manner, the gospel message is presented in striking purity. For that reason, we should magnify this ceremony as much as possible.

Make It Central

It is best for the ordinance of baptism to be observed at the beginning of the worship service or whenever the candidate is ready for baptism. It should not be tacked on at the close of the service or scheduled days or weeks from the period the candidate is ready. The baptism ceremony is worthy of our full attention because of its meaning to everyone involved.

Understanding Baptism

The importance of baptism for the Pentecostal Apostolic faith is firmly established in scripture. First, Jesus himself was baptized, setting an example for us. Matthew writes,

> *Then cometh Jesus from Galilee to Jordan unto John to be baptized of him. But John forbade him, saying, I have need to be baptized of thee, and cometh thou to me?'* And Jesus answering said unto him, *Suffer it to be so now: for thus it becometh us to fulfill all righteousness. Then he suffered him.* And Jesus, when he was baptized, went up straightway out of the water; and, lo, the heavens were *opened unto him, and he saw the Spirit of God descending like a dove, and lighting upon him: and lo a voice from heaven, saying, This is my beloved Son, in whom I am well pleased* (Matthew 3:13-17).

Second, Jesus commanded all believers to be baptized when he said, "*Go ye therefore, and teach all nations, baptizing them in the name of the Father, and of the Son, and of the Holy Ghost: teaching them to observe all things whatsoever I have commanded you: and, lo, I am with you always, even unto the end of the world*" (Matthew 27:19-20).

Third, the early church practiced baptism from its beginning. After Peter's first sermon, this commentary is made, "*Then they that gladly received his word were baptized: and the same day there were added unto them about three thousand souls. And they continued steadfastly in the apostles' doctrine and fellowship, and in breaking of bread, and in prayers*" (Acts 2:41-42). Since baptism was commanded by Christ and is so prominent in the Holy Bible, it must be important to every believer.

The Bible teaches three basic facts about baptism.

The Baptismal Committee

A baptismal committee is essential to assist the pastor in baptizing. What does this committee do?

- ✓ Plan in advance to make sure the baptistery is filled and the water is the correct temperature.
- ✓ Meet the candidates before the baptism ceremony and instruct them on the significance of baptism and the procedures of the church service.
- ✓ Take candidates to the dressing rooms and assist them in getting ready for the service. Robes and towels should be provided.
- ✓ Print the candidate's name legibly in waterproof ink on a nametag and place it on the left shoulder of the candidate so the pastor can read it. After the baptism, assist the candidates in getting dressed and caring for their wet clothes.

Baptism Ceremony

Pentecostal Apostolic churches endorse the belief that baptism is conducted by immersion in water (Matthew 3:16) and should be administered in the name of the Lord Jesus Christ for the remission of sins. The candidates shall be persons who have reached the age of accountability and understanding: baptism of infants shall not be endorsed.

The effectiveness of baptism transpires when one repents of their sins and believes the gospel with their heart. As said by one, *see, here is water; what doth hinder me to be baptized? And Philip said, If thou believest with all thine heart, thou mayest* (Acts 8:36-37). It is important not only to believe the gospel, but also, faith in the message must be followed by action-baptism. *He that believeth and is baptized shall be saved* (Mark 16:16). Hence, it is crucial that the baptism administrator carefully examines each candidate's individual belief in the gospel of grace. This gospel incorporates the death, burial, resurrection, and ascension of the Lord Jesus Christ for the remission of sins.

Baptism Formula

The candidate shall enter the water by surrendering himself or herself to the baptism administrator. The baptizer shall cross the arms of the baptism candidate across his or her chest as if giving oneself a big squeeze, offer a prayer of faith, and repeat the following:

Dearly beloved (brother/sister)—upon the confession of your faith in the death, burial, resurrection, and ascension of our Lord Jesus Christ and in the confidence which we have in the blessed word of God, I now indeed baptize you in the name of the Lord Jesus Christ for the remission of your sins; and ye shall receive the gift of the Holy Ghost. In Jesus's name! Amen.

Baptism by Immersion

The word immerse means "to submerge, to put under the water, to cover completely." When Jesus said, "Go ye therefore and teach all nations, baptizing them in the name of the Father, and of the Son, and of the Holy Ghost" (Matt. 28:19), the Greek word that he used was baptizo. It meant "to submerge, to immerse, to put under the water."

When the Bible was translated from Greek into English in 1611, almost all denominations were sprinkling for baptism. So, instead of converting the Greek word, the translators made an English word out of it by changing the "o" to an "e." It was changed from baptizo to baptize. If the Greek word had been translated correctly, the verse would have read, "Go ye therefore and immerse all nations." Other uses of this word in scripture clearly show this. In Mark 1:8 John the Baptist said, "I indeed have baptized you with water: but he shall baptize you with the Holy Ghost." He had reference to the coming of the Holy Spirit at Pentecost. Acts 1:4-5 makes that clear.

> *And, being assembled together with them, commanded them that they should not depart from Jerusalem, but wait for the promise of the Father, which, saith he, ye have heard of me. For John truly baptized with water; but ye shall be baptized with the Holy Ghost not many days hence.*

No one would suggest that those early disciples received just a sprinkling of the

Holy Ghost. They were engulfed, immersed by him.

Finally, only immersion depicts what baptism is supposed to show. Baptism is to symbolize death, burial, and resurrection. In Romans 6:3-5 Paul wrote,

> "*Know ye not, that so many of us as were baptized into Jesus Christ were baptized into his death? Therefore we are buried with him by baptism unto death: that like as Christ was raised up from the dead by the glory of the Father, even so we also should walk in newness of life. For if we have been planted together in the likeness of his death, we shall be also in the likeness of his resurrection.*"

If baptism is to identify us openly and publicly with the death, burial, and resurrection of Christ, it can best be done by immersion. We do not bury people by sprinkling dirt on them. We dig a grave and cover them up completely. So, we can best show burial by immersing people in water. In biblical baptism, the water represents a grave. When a person is lowered into the water, it identifies him with the death and burial of Jesus, and when he is raised out of the water it identifies him with his resurrection.

THE LORD'S SUPPER

Understanding The Lord's Supper

Let the world forget about the miracles that Jesus has wrought, but let them not forget his death, burial, resurrection, and ascension. By his death the gates of hell were lifted off their hinges; the foundations were cut from under the kingdom of evil; the doors of the prison house of Satan were thrown wide open. It was a day long to be remembered; it was a deed never to be forgotten.

In what manner did he seek to preserve this one immutable thing? Not by tall buildings or shafts of marble, but by two unchangeable customs: eating and drinking. As long as persons live, they must eat and drink. He chose these two things as the means of keeping alive the story of his death.

All three synoptic gospels relate the account of Jesus' observing the Last Supper (Matthew 26:26-30; Mark 14:22-26; Luke 22:14-20). The apostle Paul interprets this event when he writes,

> *For I have received of the Lord that which also I delivered unto you, That the Lord Jesus the same night in which he was betrayed took bread: And when he had given thanks, he broke it, and said, Take, eat: this is my body, which is broken for you: this do in remembrance of me. After the same manner also he took the cup, when he had supped, saying, This cup is the new testament in my blood: this do ye, as oft as ye drink it, in remembrance of me. For as often as ye eat this bread, and drink this cup, ye do shew the Lord's death till he come* (1 Corinthians 11:23-26).

Believers Only

The Lord's Supper should only be served to believers who have been baptized and filled with the Holy Spirit.

Order of Lord's Supper Service

The pastor or officiating minister moves behind the Lord's Supper table and says:

On the same night in which he was betrayed, took bread: And when he had given thanks, he broke it, and said, Take, eat; this is my body, which is broken for you: This do in remembrance of me.

The officiating minister then offers a prayer of thanks to God.

The officiating minister then nods to the deacons who are seated on the front pew. They come to the table, take a plate of bread, and serve the congregation.

While the bread is being served the organist or pianist plays appropriate music or the congregation sings a stanza of a hymn that they can recall from memory.

When the deacons complete serving they stand at the head of the pew and wait for a nod from the officiating minister. They then return to the front, place their plates on the table, and are seated or stand by the officiant.

The officiating minister then serves the deacons and returns behind the table. The minister lifts the bread for the congregation to see, and may say:

This is the bread which came down from heaven: not as the fathers ate and died; he that eateth this bread shall live forever (John 6:58).

The minister then lifts the bread to his mouth and eats it and the congregation follows.

The minister then may say:

In the same manner, also he took the cup, when he had supped, saying, This cup is the new testament in my blood: This do you as oft as ye drink it in remembrance of me.' For as often as ye eat this bread, and drink this cup, ye do show the Lord's death till he come (1 Corinthians 11:25).

The minister then offers the second prayer of thanksgiving.

The minister again nods to the deacons, who come to the table, take the cups, and serve the congregation.

The musicians play appropriate music, or the congregation sings a stanza of a hymn.

After serving the communion, the deacons should stand at the pew and wait for a nod from the minister. They then return to the front, place the trays on the table and are seated or stand by the minister.

The minister then serves the deacons and returns behind the table. The minister then lifts his cup so everyone can see it and may say:

"*... all things are by the law purged with blood; and without shedding of blood is no remission*" (Hebrews 9:22). "*But if we walk in the light, as he is in the light, we have fellowship one with another, and the blood of Jesus Christ his Son cleanseth us from all sin*" (1 John 1:7).

The minister then lifts the cup to his lips and drinks. The congregation follows.

The minister then places the cup back on the table and could sing a hymn.

(The Blood Will Never Lose Its Power)

(Joy to the World)

Variations in the Lord's Supper

The Lord's Supper can be carried out in variety manner. In every instance, however, it should be served with reverence and dignity. When and how often it is observed is a matter of choice for each church.

MARRIAGE CEREMONY

Marriage Laws And Information

Marriage is an institution ordained by God, and ministers should be cautious to ascertain the legal qualification of any parties desiring to be married by them. The process shall not be taken lightly or unadvisedly. Before any minister consecrates a marriage, they should be knowledgeable of the state's existing marriage laws. In some states, it is required that the minister acquire a state license—a number which must be recorded on every marriage certificate issued to them. In other states, a license must be delivered to the couple before the marriage ceremony. The authority issuing the license as well as the contracting parties must obtain a copy of the marriage certificate. Also, for legal purposes, a careful minister will file a personal copy for necessary reference.

If a marriage ceremony is performed without a legal warrant, the marriage will be valid, but the minister will be subject to fine and imprisonment.

The following marriage ceremony is an outline and may or may not be used at the discretion of the officiating minister. However, it is important to assure that such an important contract has appropriate and religious significance.

The marriage requires careful planning and adequate preparation. To this end, the minister should arrange for at least two prenuptial consultations with the bride and groom, one to discuss the wedding and the other to discuss the marriage.

In the first session, a detailed discussion should be about the host church's policies governing weddings, appropriate music, favorite scriptures, etc. In the second, counsel should be given to the bride and groom about the importance and specifics of marriage. Subjects such as family finances, the importance of religious faith, in-law relations, personality differences, and the physical side of marriage should be thoroughly discussed. The couple should be reminded that the wedding will last only about 30 minutes, hopefully, the marriage will last a lifetime. Both need careful and prayerful planning.

The essential element of every marriage ceremony is the mutual agreement of the parties to accept each other as husband and wife. Furthermore, society has a right to know that the parties have mutually contracted to live together as husband and wife.

Any marriage or civil union between two males or two females is in violation of and is condemned by the Word of God. Likewise, the Holy Scripture has clearly directed all believers to abstain from all forms of fornication (1 Thessalonians 4:3). However, if anyone shall forsake and renounce their ungodly relationship, repent, be baptized in the name of Jesus Christ, and be filled with the Holy Spirit, they can be delivered from these relationships solely by the power of God.

ORDER OF THE WEDDING SERVICE

Forty-five minutes before the wedding begins, the organist (or pianist) and ushers arrive. The music is played softly, and the ushers greet and seat the people as they arrive. If several ladies enter together, the eldest should be escorted by the usher.

Five minutes before the ceremony begins, the candles are lit. They may be lit earlier if the lighting is not a part of the ceremony.

Two minutes before the ceremony begins, the father and mother of the groom are seated on the second row, right (See Diagram).

One minute before the ceremony begins, the mother of the bride is seated on the second row, left (see diagram below).

Divorce has become so commonplace that stepparents are frequently in attendance. Normally, stepparents should be accorded the same courtesies as grandparents, usually seated near the front of the church behind the parents. If a divorced father is giving his daughter in marriage and his present wife is in attendance, she should be seated in front of the mother of the groom and behind the row on which the mother of the bride is seated. During your premarital counseling, you should determine if relationships between divorced persons are such that an extra row should separate the father of the bride and his wife from the mother of the bride (and her husband).

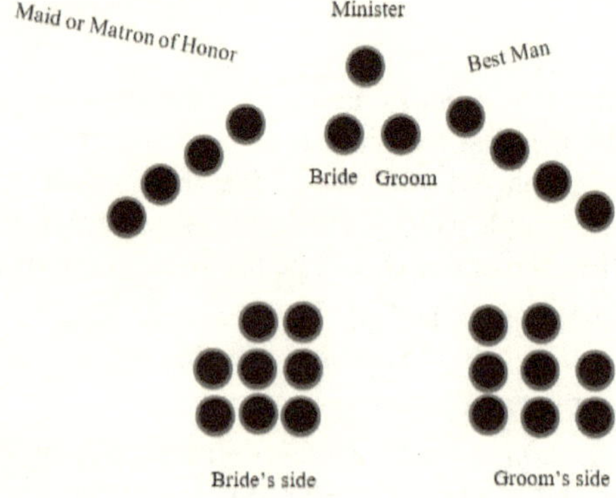

If the father of the bride is deceased or divorced, the bride may want a stepfather, brother, uncle, or even a friend to give her in marriage. Or, she may choose to omit this custom entirely.

At the appointed time to begin, the special music is presented.

After the special music, the minister leads the groom and best man and groomsmen in from the side entrance.

When the groomsmen are in place, the bridesmaids enter down the aisle, followed by the maid or matron of honor. Small pieces of tape on the floor may be used to mark where the attendants are to stand.

The bride enters on the left arm of her father. The mother may lead the congregation by standing as the bride enters. The bride and her father walk to the minister and stop. The minister makes some introductory remarks and then asks, "Who gives this woman to be married?" The father replies, "Her mother and I do."

The father turns and is seated next to his wife, and the groom steps up to take his place.

The ceremony begins.

When the ceremony is over, the bride and groom lead the recessional.

An usher escorts the parents of the bride out and then the parents of the groom. Grandparents may also be escorted out if they are present, followed by stepparents.

The minister may invite the guests to the reception and dismisses the congregation.

The Traditional Marriage Ceremony

Addressing all gathered, the minister faces both the couple and the congregation, the bride on the right and the groom on the left of the minister:

THE INTRODUCTORY PRAYER

Dearly beloved, we are gathered together here in the sight of God and in the presence of these witnesses to join together this man and this woman in holy matrimony. Instituted by God in the time of man's innocence, marriage is an honorable and holy estate which Christ adorned with His presence and first miracle that He wrought in Cana of Galilee. This miracle, which Holy Scripture commends to be honored among all people, signifies unto us the mystical union that exists between Christ and His church.

God intends this same union of husband and wife for the couple's mutual joy; the help and comfort have given each other in prosperity and adversity; and, when it is God's will, for the procreation of children and their nurture in the knowledge and love of the Lord.

Therefore, matrimony is not to be entered unto unadvisedly, but reverently, discreetly, and in the fear of God.

THE INTERROGATION

The minister shall charge the congregation with the following words:

(Bride's name) and (groom's name) have now come to be joined into this holy estate. Therefore, if anyone can show just cause why they should not lawfully be joined together, let them speak now, or else hereafter forever hold their peace.

The minister shall speak to the couple the following words:

I require and charge you both, here in the presence of God and the witness of this company, that if either of you know of any impediments why ye may not lawfully be joined together in matrimony, do now confess it. Furthermore, be well assured that if any persons are joined otherwise than as God's word doth allow, they are not joined by God and neither is their marriage lawful.

If there is an alleged impediment from any member of the congregation then, it is best the

minister stops the ceremony and removes the two parties to his office for discussion.

If no impediments shall be alleged, the minister shall say to the groom the following words:

Mr. (groom's name), will you take Ms. (bride's name), to be your wedded wife, to live together after God's ordinance in the holy estate of matrimony? Will you love her, comfort her, honor her, and keep her, in sickness and in health; and, forsaking all other, be faithful unto her as long as you both shall live?

The groom shall answer, "*I will*".

The minister shall say to the bride the following words:

Ms. (bride's name), will you take Mr. (groom's name), to be your wedded husband, to live together after God's ordinance in the holy estate of matrimony? Will you love him, serve him, honor him, and keep him, in sickness and in health; and, forsaking all other, be faithful unto him as long as you both shall live?

The bride shall answer, "*I will*".

The minister addresses the congregation, saying:

Will all of you witnessing these promises do all in prayer and in support to uphold this couple in their marriage?

The congregation responds, "*We will*"

THE PRESENTATION

The minister shall say:

Who giveth this woman to be married to this man?

The bride's father or representative

"*Her mother and I do*" or "*She gives herself, with the blessing of her mother and father*".

(A hymn, song, or reading may follow)

THE VOWS

The groom faces the bride and takes her right hand in his.

Since you have expressed a desire to be united in marriage, I am going to ask you to take a vow—a vow that is made not only in the presence of your family and friends, but also in the presence of God. The Bible makes it clear that God is a witness to the wedding vows. I believe he is an unseen guest here today. He hears the vows you make and he intends that they are kept so long as you both shall live.

The minister, after receiving the bride at her father or loved one's hand, shall direct the groom to join his right hand to the right hand of his bride and repeat the following words:

In the name of the Lord, I (groom's name), *take thee (bride's name), to be my wedded wife, to have and to hold from this day forward. For better, for worse, for richer, for poorer, in sickness and in health, to love and to cherish, till death do we part, according to God's holy ordinance; thereto I plight thee my troth.*

They drop hands.

The minister shall direct the bride to take his right hand in hers, then says the following words:

In the name of the Lord Jesus, I (bride's name), take thee (groom's name), to be my wedded husband, to have and to hold from this day forward. For better, for worse, for richer, for poorer, in sickness and in health, to love and to cherish, till death do we part, according to God's holy ordinance; thereto I plight thee my troth.

They drop hands.

THE BLESSING AND EXCHANGE OF RINGS

If this is a ring ceremony, at this time the minister shall receive the rings and ask God's blessing on the rings.

The minister shall ask the groom:

(Groom's name), what do you give as a token of your love for (bride's name)?

The best man, acting for the groom, hands the ring to the minister.

The minister shall say:

(Groom's name), since ancient time the ring has been used to seal important covenants. Since the earliest of times and parliaments unknown, the great seals of state were fixed on rings worn by the reigning monarch, and its stamp was the sole sign of imperial authority. In later years, in the days of the legendary King Arthur and his Knights of the Round Table, friends often exchanged simple bands of gold as enduring evidences of friendships

and good will. But today, the ring has gained a far deeper meaning. It has become symbolic of a man's love for a woman and of a woman's love for a man.

(Groom's name), you will notice that this ring is a complete circle, without beginning or end. It is symbolic, I trust, of the endlessness of your love for (bride).

The minister then hands the bride's ring to the groom and shall say:

(Groom), you will take the ring, place it on the third finger of (bride)'s left hand, and as you place it there repeat after me, "With this ring I thee wed, and all my worldly goods. I thee endow. In the name of the Lord, Jesus Christ. Amen."

The minister then asks the bride:

And, (bride), what do you give as a token of your love for (groom)?

The maid or matron of honor, acting for the bride, hands the groom's ring to the minister.

The minister shall say:

(Bride's name), you will notice that this ring is made of the purest of metals. It will not turn or tarnish with age. It is symbolic, I trust, of the purity of your love for (groom's name). You will take the ring, place it on the third finger of (groom)'s left hand, and as you place it there, repeat after me: "With this ring. I thee wed and all my worldly goods. I thee endow. In the name of the Lord, Jesus Christ. Amen."

The minister joins the bride's right hand and the groom's right hand, and say:

These rings are very precious. First, they are made of precious metal, which symbolizes that your love is the most precious element in each other's lives. Secondly, from the earliest of times, the circle has been a symbol of completeness; a symbol of wholeness. It has no beginning nor ending unless broken by an outside force. This unbroken and never-ending circle symbolizes your commitment of love that is never ending. Finally, the wedding ring on the ring finger represents your fidelity to one another. These rings will represent the infinite love between the two of you. When either of you looks at this symbol, I hope that you will be reminded of these commitments to one another, which you make today.

Dear Father, bless, O Lord, these rings as a symbol of the vows by which this man and this woman have bound themselves to each other through Jesus Christ, our Lord. God, may they live in your grace and be forever true to this union. Amen.

All: *Amen.*

Prayer

The minister shall say:

"Entreat me not to leave you, or to turn back from following after you; For wherever you go, I will go; and wherever you lodge, I will lodge;

Your people shall be my people, and your God, my God."

Then the minister joins the bride's right hand and the groom's right hand, and shall say:

Now that (bride's name) and (groom's name) have given themselves to each other by solemn vows, with the joining of hands and the giving and receiving of rings, I pronounce that they are husband and wife, in the name of the Lord, Jesus Christ.

All: "*Amen.*"

CONCLUDING PRAYERS

(If there is a visiting minister, they may be called on to say this prayer).

The minister directs the congregation to stand, saying:

Let us all stand and recite the Lord's Prayer together:

Our Father, who art in heaven, hallowed be thy Name. Thy kingdom come, thy will be done, on earth as it is in heaven. Give us this day our daily bread, and forgive us our trespasses, as we forgive those who trespass against us. And lead us not into temptation, but deliver us from evil, for thine is the kingdom, and the power, and the glory, forever. Amen. (Matthew 6:9-13)

The officiating minister then directs the congregation to sit, the couple to kneel, and the service continues with prayers or song.

The officiant minister blesses the kneeling couple, saying:

God, our Father, who richly gives his Holy Spirit to whosoever will ask, may He bless you and keep you. The Lord make his face shine upon you, and be gracious unto you.

May, the Lord lift up his countenance upon you, and give you peace.

May, the Lord mercifully with his favor look upon you, and fill you with all spiritual blessings and grace; that you may faithfully live together in this life. Blessed be the God and Father of our Lord, who hath blessed us with all spiritual blessings in heavenly places in Christ Jesus. Amen.

The minister addresses all gathered:

The peace of the Lord be with you always.

The bride and groom stand and face each other. The minister speaks:

(Bride's name) and (groom's name), having witnessed your vows of love to one another, it is my joy to present you to all gathered here as husband and wife. (To the groom.) You may kiss the bride.

THE PRONOUNCEMENT

The minister shall say:

By the pleasure of God, and the approval of family and friends, I bid this marriage to prosper in God's grace.

(Groom's name) and (bride's name) have consented together in holy matrimony and have witnessed the same before God and this company. They have given and pledged their troth to each other and have declared the same by giving and

receiving a ring. Therefore, I, (minister's name), a minister of the Gospel of Jesus Christ and with the power vested in me in the State of _____, pronounce that they are man and wife. What therefore God hath joined together, let not man put asunder. Amen.

Ladies and gentlemen, I present to you Mr. and Mrs. (groom's last name).

The couple kisses and exits.

The minister follows the wedding party for the congratulatory portion of the celebration for the bride and the groom.

Variations For Wedding Ceremonies

While the core elements of every wedding ceremony should include the same components (a Christian message, sacred vows, and the exchange of rings) there is room for variety. The minister should strive to make each wedding as personal and as unique as possible. Here are some ways to add variety to the standard wedding ceremony.

SIGNING THE BIBLE

The minister may, if the bride and groom desire, have an open Bible placed on a table on the platform. After he pronounces them husband and wife, he may then say:

"(Groom) and (bride), would you now sign the Bible as a testimony of your commitment here today?"

The groom and bride then step to the table, each person signs the Bible; the minister then says:

(Groom) you may kiss your wife.

UNITY CANDLE

The minister may, if the bride and groom wish, have three candles placed on a table on the platform. The two outside candles are lit before the beginning of the service. Following the pronouncement of the couple as husband and wife, the minister shall say:

(Groom) and (bride), the Bible teaches that in marriage the two become one flesh. In the symbolism of this, will you now light the unity candle?

The couple steps to the table, each takes one of the lighted candles, and together they light the center candle. They then extinguish their candles and place them back in the stands.

The minister then says:

(Groom) you may kiss your wife.

AS AN OPENING

The minister may, with the couple's agreement, have them turn around and face the congregation immediately before the beginning of the traditional ceremony. He may then say:

This congregation is made up of people who have played a vital part in your lives. They are your parents, your family, and your friends. They have come here out of a sense of love and warmth of heart. They are your roots, the flowering of your years. As you turn to speak the words that will unite your lives, be mindful of those behind you, and know that in good days or bad, you will never be alone.

Then have the couple turn to the minister again and begin the ceremony.

Reaffirmation Of Wedding Vows

Submitted By the Late Bishop Francis L. Smith

The officiating minister should stand before the congregation and the couple to reaffirm and say the following words:

Dear friends, God has smiled on this couple that has enjoyed love, friendship, and material harmony by the grace of God for many years. They have come now to reaffirm the vows, which they created and declared (#) year(s) ago.

(Husband's name) and (wife's name), it is a pleasure to share today's very special occasion with you.

Many people believe that entering into marriage is the final step in a romantic relationship. As they see it, a couple meets, gets to know each other, falls in love, decides they want to go through life together, and then take the final step—marriage.

But marriage is not meant to be the final step in a couple's relationship. Instead, it is really just the beginning of a grand adventure which, hopefully, will be long and fruitful.

You have shared the joys, blessings, and yes, the challenges, of married life for (#) year(s) already. Now, today you both wish to reconfirm your commitment of working together to make your marriage grow and blossom in the years yet to come. May this ceremony, renewing the vows you took to become husband and wife on your wedding day, remind you that despite the stresses inevitable in every life, your love, respect, trust and understanding of each other will continue to increase your contentment and heighten your joy in living.

Please join hands.

The officiating minister shall speak to the couple the following words:

Mr. (husband's name) and Mrs. (wife's name), by the very fact, that you have presented yourselves here, we know that your intention is to continue in the state of matrimony for as long as the Lord will permit. Therefore, we await your statement of reaffirmation.

The officiating minister shall say to the man the following words:

Mr. (husband's name), will you take Mrs. (wife's name) hand and say these words to her?

I, (husband's name), have accepted you (wife's name), as a gift from God. I love you with a love that only God could put into my heart. Will you continue to have (wife's name) as your wife and continue to live in this marriage?

The husband shall answer: "I will".

Do you reaffirm your love for her, and will you love her, honor her, and cherish her in sickness and in health, for richer or poorer, for better for worse, and forsaking all others, be faithful to her as long as you both shall live?

The husband shall answer: "I will".

The officiating minister shall say to the woman the following words:

Mrs. (wife's name), will you take Mr. (husband's name) hand and say these words to him?

I, (wife's name), have accepted you (husband's name), as a gift from God. I love you with a love that only God could put into my heart. Will you continue to have (husband's name) as your husband and continue to live in this marriage?

The wife shall answer: "I will".

Do you reaffirm your love for him, and will you love him, honor him, and cherish him in sickness and in health, for richer or poorer, for better for worse, and forsaking all others, be faithful to him as long as you both shall live?

The wife shall answer: "I will".

Scriptural Reading from Corinthians: (any variety of readings can be substituted here)

Love endures and is kind.
Love is not envious or jealous.
Love wants not for itself.
Love is not puffed up, nor does it behave wrongly.
Love seeks not for its own.
Love is not easily provoked.
Love is not rude.
Love thinks no evil.
Love does not rejoice in wrong, but dwells in the truth.
Love bears all things, believes all things, endures all things, and love never fails.

If there is to be a ring ceremony, it comes at this point. The minister shall take the ring from the woman, deliver it unto the man, and direct him to place it upon the ring finger of the woman's left hand. Holding the ring there, and repeating after the minister, the man shall say the following words:

On your wedding day, you exchanged rings as a symbol of the never-ending circle of love. Rings serve as a reminder of your wedding vows to each other, and your commitment to live in unity and happiness, yielding love for each other. At this time, it is appropriate to reconfirm the meaning of the rings you wear.

With this ring, I (husband's name) reaffirm my vows to love, cherish, and protect you, and give myself only to you as a husband, so long as we both shall live.

With this ring, I (wife's name) reaffirm my vows to love, cherish, and protect you, and give myself only to you as a wife, so long as we both shall live.

If there is a visiting minister, he may be called on to pray.

The officiating minister shall say:

By the pleasure of God, and the approval of family and friends, I bless this marriage to continue and prosper in God's grace. Ladies and gentlemen, I give you again, Mr. and Mrs. (name).

WEDDING RECORD

Name of Bride and Groom	Wedding Date
1. ____________________	
____________________	____________________
2. ____________________	
____________________	____________________
3. ____________________	
____________________	____________________
4. ____________________	
____________________	____________________
5. ____________________	
____________________	____________________
6. ____________________	
____________________	____________________
7. ____________________	
____________________	____________________
8. ____________________	
____________________	____________________
9. ____________________	
____________________	____________________
10. ____________________	
____________________	____________________
11. ____________________	
____________________	____________________
12. ____________________	
____________________	____________________

13. ______________

______________ ______________

14. ______________

______________ ______________

15. ______________

______________ ______________

16. ______________

______________ ______________

17. ______________

______________ ______________

18. ______________

______________ ______________

19. ______________

______________ ______________

20. ______________

______________ ______________

21. ______________

______________ ______________

22. ______________

______________ ______________

23. ______________

______________ ______________

24. ______________

______________ ______________

25. ____________________

____________________ ____________________

26. ____________________

____________________ ____________________

27. ____________________

____________________ ____________________

28. ____________________

____________________ ____________________

29. ____________________

____________________ ____________________

30. ____________________

____________________ ____________________

31. ____________________

____________________ ____________________

32. ____________________

____________________ ____________________

33. ____________________

____________________ ____________________

34. ____________________

____________________ ____________________

35. ____________________

____________________ ____________________

36. ____________________

____________________ ____________________

37. ____________________

____________________ ____________________

38. ____________________

____________________ ____________________

39. ____________________

____________________ ____________________

40. ____________________

____________________ ____________________

41. ____________________

____________________ ____________________

42. ____________________

____________________ ____________________

43. ____________________

____________________ ____________________

44. ____________________

____________________ ____________________

45. ____________________

____________________ ____________________

46. ____________________

____________________ ____________________

47. ____________________

____________________ ____________________

48. ____________________

____________________ ____________________

49. ____________________

____________________ ____________________

50. ____________________

____________________ ____________________

51. ____________________

____________________ ____________________

52. ____________________

____________________ ____________________

53. ____________________

____________________ ____________________

54. ____________________

____________________ ____________________

55. ____________________

____________________ ____________________

56. ____________________

____________________ ____________________

57. ____________________

____________________ ____________________

58. ____________________

____________________ ____________________

59. ____________________

____________________ ____________________

60. ____________________

____________________ ____________________

61. ____________________

____________________ ____________________

62. ____________________

____________________ ____________________

63. ____________________

____________________ ____________________

64. ____________________

____________________ ____________________

65. ____________________

____________________ ____________________

66. ____________________

____________________ ____________________

67. ____________________

____________________ ____________________

FUNERAL ETIQUETTE

Etiquette And Clergy Courtesy For Funerals

Contributed by the late Bishop Francis L. Smith

Pastors are representatives of Christ; they are not vicars. They are subject to error and mistakes but are to be conscious of their representation of Christ at all times and in all places. Funerals are very sensitive times for the families and friends left behind. During the time of a funeral, pastors need to meet with the families to help fulfill their individual needs.

1. Meeting with the family

   a. Help make funeral arrangements

   b. Help make decisions about funeral cost.

2. Meeting with the mortician

   a. Acquaint yourself with the procedure and practices of the locality such as times for internment, the cost for overtime, etc.

b. Be familiar with the terms of the director and work together for a smoothly run service.

3. Planning the service

a. Assist the family in making the service one of simplicity, dignity, and sincerity.

b. Assist to minimize family pain. Service should be according to the pastor's concept. Guide them to accomplish the purpose you have in mind.

4. Pulpit etiquette

• Acknowledge the presence of other ministers, even if they are unknown to you. They may be invited to the pulpit. Do not insult people by ignoring other pastors.

5. Changing trends in funeral services

a. Evening funeral services:

The order of funerals today is more pagan, neither Christian nor biblical (study Acts 5). Between funerals, the pastor should teach his congregation the truth of the gospel, that there may be a better understanding of funeralizing people.

b. Calling or viewing hour should always precede the funeral and committal at an evening funeral service with the body buried the next morning. The pastor may or may not accompany the ceremony, but it would be best for him to be there to do what is best for the family.

Importance Of The Funeral Service

There are various responsibilities presented to the minister at the planning of a church member's funeral. They may be viewed as challenges or may offer a great opportunity to minister. During these times, many people look to God and are more open to Him than at any other time in their lives. When the funeral service is conducted correctly, the minister becomes an instrument of the Lord to bring God and people together. In this instance, the funeral becomes a powerful means of ministry.

A funeral service provides an opportunity to do three essential things:

1.) An Opportunity to Heal

Primarily, a funeral is an opportunity to heal the brokenhearted. That was an important part of Jesus' ministry, and it should be a vital part of yours (Luke 4:18-19). As someone has said, the minister has a two-fold task—to comfort the disturbed and to disturb the comfortable. Funerals are meaningful because they provide an opportunity to give comfort to the living.

2.) An Opportunity to Give Hope

Secondarily, a funeral is a time to proclaim our hope in Jesus Christ. A funeral service provides an opportunity to present the gospel to more lost people than any other single occasion. Rightly conducted, it becomes an opportunity for both sowing and reaping.

3.) An Opportunity to Honor

Finally, it provides an opportunity to honor the dead and to affirm the value of life. The Bible tells us that we are made in the likeness of God. That fact alone gives dignity and worth to every person, regardless of who they are or what they have done.

The ritual, the friends, the flowers, the music, and the word of God all make the funeral service a paramount means of accomplishing healing, the giving of hope, and the paying of honor.

What to Do When Someone Dies?

At times your presence will be more needed and appreciated. In those moments, you will be able to touch people more deeply and meaningfully than at death. People will soon forget the sermons you preach, the buildings you build, or the awards you receive. But, they will never forget that you came quickly when notified of a death, and buried their mother or father, their husband or wife, or their child. Being with people and ministering to them during such times builds bonds that last a lifetime.

Call the home as soon as you learn of the death and ask when would be a convenient time to visit. Unless a specific time is stated, go immediately if possible. For many people, you represent God. Your presence will be a source of strength and comfort to them. And, they will not need you more than they need you then.

What will you say when you get there? A warm handshake, a gentle hug, a pat on the shoulder, and the simple words, "God bless you, (name)," is enough.

Words mean very little. Above all, avoid trite and empty chatter. Your presence is enough. It says, "I care." It says, "God cares." It says, "You matter." It says, "You are not alone. We are here to help you through this."

Listen. Let the person talk and make mental notes of what they say and write them down as soon as you get back to your car. They will give you important information about the life and the death of the deceased. Some of these things you will want to incorporate into the funeral sermon to make it more personal.

You need not stay long—15-30 minutes is sufficient. When the time is right, ask if you can lead in prayer. After the prayer, assure the family you will return later to talk about funeral arrangements.

Alert the proper people in your church. The deceased's Sunday School class, deacons in charge of ministry to the bereaved, those who provide food, to make sure they know what has happened.

Return later for a second visit. As you visit with the closest relatives of the deceased, you might ask if there are favorite verses or hymns they would like used in the funeral service. Usually, without asking, they will share with you interesting and pertinent facts concerning the deceased.

This time you need not make mental notes, you can write down things they say. Sometimes it is not a bad idea to use the deceased's Bible in the funeral service. Often, as you thumb through it, you will find passages marked, clippings from newspapers, poems, and even quotes you may want to use in the funeral service. When the deceased's Bible is used in the service it may be presented to the family at the cemetery.

Though you will never get accustomed to it and never feel fully adequate, go to people in their hours of deepest sorrow, and they will thank you throughout all eternity.

Preparation of the Funeral Sermon

At the outset of his earthly ministry Jesus stood in the synagogue in Nazareth and read from Isaiah the prophet, "The Spirit of the Lord is upon me, because he hath anointed me to preach deliverance to the captives and recovering of sight to the blind, to set at liberty them that are bruised, to preach the acceptable year of the Lord" (Luke 14:18-19).

If ministers today are to be true to their calling, they must make Jesus' priorities their priorities.

And high on this list must be the work of "healing the broken-hearted."

How do we do this? In many ways. We do it, in part, through ministering to people in times of sorrow and death. And, primarily through the funeral sermon. This is no easy assignment for several reasons.

First, it is because we must deal with people in the most traumatic time of their lives. Second, death often comes with such short notice that there is little time to prepare the funeral message in advance. With all the funeral demands placed upon a minister and such a short time to prepare, the minister may be tempted to muddle through the sermon.

Somehow, the busy minister must find time to prepare and preach effective funeral messages. I think this approach would help any minister—especially young ministers. Here are several basic suggestions that I offer concerning the preparation of funeral sermons.

Be Biblical. Primarily, be biblical. The question of the ages was first posed by Job, "If a man die, shall he live again?" (Job 14:14). Through the years persons have sought to find an answer to that question in science, in nature, and in human reason. The only certain word, however, concerning life after death, comes from God's word. The only real assurance there is of life after death rests in the death, burial, and resurrection of Jesus Christ. Because he lives, we shall live also.

Be Personal. Secondarily, be personal. The minister should take time to talk with the family of the deceased before the funeral and learn something about him/her. Every person is special and unique. You can learn something about the birth, work, background, character, or age of the deceased by visiting with the family. This will allow you to add a personal word about them. A few well-chosen personal remarks can transform a cold, formal message into a warm, personal word of comfort and hope.

A word of caution, however. Don't talk too much about the deceased. Focus mostly on Jesus Christ. He is our hope and our comforter.

Be Brief. Third, be brief. The funeral service should be characterized by orderliness, simplicity, and brevity. A well-prepared message can say all that needs to be said and can be absorbed by a grieving family in 10 to 15 minutes.

If we are to fulfill our calling as ministers, a part of which is to heal the broken-hearted, we must become masters of the craft of funeral sermons. Our ministry to the bereaved is too great to be taken lightly.

Identification. It is appropriate to identify with those who grieve. In some cases, you will conduct a service where you are connected to the deceased. But be careful that the funeral message does not become a time to transfer your feelings—especially something dredged up from your childhood—onto the family and congregation. You may need to find a trusted counselor to resolve your grief, but for now, you have other work to do. You have come to minister and not to be served.

Suggested Funeral Sermon Texts

Sample scripture for the funeral of a saint

Job 14:14; Psalm 23; Psalm 73:24-26; Psalm 116:15; John 5:25-29; John 11:14-26; John 14:1-6; 1 Corinthians 15:50-58; 2 Corinthians 1:3-7; 2 Corinthians 5:1-10; 2 Timothy 4:6-8; Revelation 14:13; Revelation 21:1-6; Revelation 22:1-5

Sample scripture for the funeral of a non-Christian

Psalm 1; Psalm 39:4-7; Psalm 46:1-5; Psalm 90; Psalm 103:13-17

Sample scripture for the funeral of a godly woman

Proverbs 30:10-30

Sample scripture for the funeral of a little child

2 Samuel 12:18-23; Matthew 5:22-24, 35-40; Matthew 18:1-6; Matthew 18:10-14; Mark 10:13-16; Luke 7:11-15

Sample scripture for the funeral of a suicide

Habakkuk 3:17-19; Romans 8:35-39; 2 Corinthians 12:9-10

After the Funeral Is Over

The minister who is interested in "healing the broken-hearted" soon realizes that his work is not finished when he has preached the funeral sermon or conducted the graveside service. Grief goes on and so must our ministry to the grieving.

What can the minister say and do at such a time that will be helpful to the family? There is no one dramatic gesture or pearl of wisdom that will dissolve the heartache, but there are many acts of ministry that can convey your concern and help to soften the blow that the person has suffered.

Reach Out to Them. Be there! Words may not be the primary need of grieving people, but simply, your presence is what counts. "There is still nothing more powerful than one human being reaching out to another."

Help them understand their grief. Grief is a person's reaction to a loss. The more meaningful the loss, the more intense the grief. Many people, when they experience grief, wonder what's happening to them. When there comes a numbness of spirit, the loss of memory, the trembling of limbs, tears are released uncontrollably. The griever can't sleep and feels anxious, fear, anger, and guilt.

Learn to Listen. Be a good listener. For most people, talking is an effective means of releasing emotions and undergoing healing. So, listen! The process will have a greater impact than anything else you can do.

As people grief they may ask, "Why, God?" "Why did this happen to me?" Don't be a superficial Bible quoter. Simplistic answers to complex questions are not only unhelpful, but they can also harmful. Statements like, "This is God's will," or "God knows best," are theologically shallow and provide little or no comfort. It is better to hear their questions as cries of pain rather than literal questions. And don't attempt to tell the bereaved how he/she feels. To say, "I know how you feel" is presumptuous unless someone has told you his feelings.

Emotional First Aid

Grief resembles steam in a steam engine; unless it can escape in a controlled way, pressure builds up and the boiler explodes.

One way to express grief is through tears. There is a Jewish proverb that says, "What soap is to the body, tears are to the soul." Tears can help cleanse the soul.

What Can Wait, Should

Fifth, encourage the postponement of major decisions during a period of grief. Grieving people need to realize that no matter how they feel at the moment, their feelings will change. So, whatever can wait should wait until after the period of intense grief.

Comfort the Children

Don't ignore the children of the family. Children, because of their limited experience, may not understand all that has happened when a loved one dies, but don't assume that a seemingly calm child is not sorrowing. Children do grieve and they grieve deeply. A child's feelings are worthy of respect. Jesus took time for little children and so should we.

Use the Lay People

Encourage church members to visit and help. Among life's greatest blessings in times of grief are friends and fellow church members. They are often instruments of God's grace. Since a minister has many people to minister to, he should enlist, train, and encourage his people to join him in ministering to the grieving.

Grief is Major Surgery

Stay in touch! Grieving takes a long time. Exactly how long depends on the circumstances of the loss, the depth of the relationship, and the emotional makeup of the one grieving. It is not unusual for it to last a year or more. The loss that causes grief is major surgery. The healing takes time.

One way to stay in touch is by mail. When I was a pastor I made a practice each Christmas and New Year season of writing a note to each member of my congregation who had lost a loved one during the year. Holidays are the worst times of the year for grieving people, and Christmas is the hardest of all the holidays.

A good practice is to mark next year's calendar and visit the family on the exact anniversary of either the death or the funeral.

The Funeral Service

If the department is brought in by way of a processional, the officiating minister, while walking ahead, shall say the following words:

> *I am the resurrection, and the life: he that believeth in me, though he were dead, yet shall*
>
> *he live: and whosoever liveth and believeth in me shall never die (John 11:25-26).*
>
> *For we know that if our earthly house of this tabernacle were dissolved, we have a*
>
> *building of God, a house not made with hands, eternal in the heavens*
>
> *(2 Corinthians 5:1).*
>
> *For we brought nothing into this world, and it is certain we can carry nothing out*
>
> *(1 Timothy 6:7).*
>
> *The Lord gave, and the Lord hath taken away; blessed be the name of the Lord*

(Job 1:21).

At this point, while the people are gathering, it is appropriate to read either the twenty-third or the ninety-third Psalm.

The scriptural reading may be followed by a suitable hymn.

At this time, the officiating minister or host pastor may offer prayer or choose a visiting minister to do so.

Proceed with the following recommendations if there is no formal program:

Following the prayer of comfort, the obituary and acknowledgments may be read.

Selected solo's or choir songs may be rendered at this time.

The host pastor or a designated minister shall deliver the eulogy.

The Gravesite

Once at the gravesite, the officiating minister should stand at the head of the grave and wait until all of the people have gathered under the tent. During this time, to help draw in all minds, it is good to have a short prayer by the officiating minister, pastor, or designated minister.

Then the minister shall say:

Lord, make me to know mine end, and the measure of my days, what it is: that I may know how frail I am (Psalms 39:4). In the midst of life we are in death: of whom may we seek for comfort, but of thee O Lord, whom for our sins art justly displeased?

Man that is born of a woman is of few days and full of trouble. He cometh forth like a flower, and is cut down: he fleeth also as a shadow, and continueth not (Job 14:1-2). Thou knowest, Lord, the secrets of our hearts; shut not thy mercy ears to our prayer.

Funeral attendants will occasionally cast earth upon the departed during the officiating minister's final words:

For as much as the spirit of the departed hath returned to the God who gave it, we therefore commit his/her body to the ground. Earth to earth, ashes to ashes, dust to dust. Looking for the coming of the Lord when He himself shall descend from heaven with a shout, with the voice of the Archangel, and with the trump of God; and the dead in Christ shall rise first. Then we who are still alive and remain shall be caught up together with them in the clouds, to meet the Lord in the air; so shall we ever be with the Lord.

I heard a voice from heaven saying unto me, write, blessed are the dead which die in the Lord from henceforth: Yea, saith the Spirit, that they may rest from their labors; and their works do follow them (Revelation 14:13).

At the conclusion of the home-going service, the officiating minister or visiting minister may offer this prayer:

The grace of our Lord Jesus Christ and the love of God and the communion of the Holy Spirit be with you all forevermore, amen.

What To Do At The Cemetery

When the casket has been placed over the grave and the family is seated, the minister may say: We have now done all we can do for our friend, (deceased). "We have brought his/her body to its final resting place. We now commend their body to the earth from whence it came."

I read again from the word of God. Some relevant passages are Psalm 23, 1 Thessalonians 4:13-18, Revelation 21:1-7, or Psalm 1.

You may then ask the people to bow for prayer and say: "This prayer will conclude the services."

Following the prayer, shake hands with family members and move out from under the canopy.

By custom, the minister stands near the head of the casket. Funeral directors almost always tell you which end is the head.

Military Ceremonies

If full military rites are granted, you can be sure a noncommissioned officer will be present to conduct this impressive ceremony. After the rifle salute and bugle taps, the military will fold the flag and present it to the widow or children or mother. You may open the graveside service, make your remarks, then offer a benediction after the delivery of the flag.

More often, a veteran may have an official flag on his or her casket without military personnel in attendance. In this situation, the funeral director will fold the flag and present it to you. You may then offer it to the chosen family member with the words: "(name of the deceased's family member), I have the high privilege of representing the President of the United States in presenting to you this flag in appreciation by the Commander in Chief for the service of your (husband, son, father, brother, mother, daughter, wife, sister) in defense of our country." Then offer any closing remarks and the benediction.

Bad Weather

In cold or rainy weather, it is a kindness to ask men at graveside to wear their hats for the service.

FUNERAL RECORD

	Name of Deceased	Date of Funeral	Sermon Text
1.			
2.			
3.			
4.			
5.			
6.			
7.			
8.			
9.			
10.			
11.			
12.			
13.			
14.			
15.			
16.			
17.			
18.			
19.			
20.			
21.			
22.			
23.			
24.			
25.			

26. ______________________________
27. ______________________________
28. ______________________________
29. ______________________________
30. ______________________________
31. ______________________________
32. ______________________________
33. ______________________________
34. ______________________________
35. ______________________________
36. ______________________________
37. ______________________________
38. ______________________________
39. ______________________________
40. ______________________________
41. ______________________________
42. ______________________________
43. ______________________________
44. ______________________________
45. ______________________________
46. ______________________________
47. ______________________________
48. ______________________________
49. ______________________________
50. ______________________________
51. ______________________________
52. ______________________________
53. ______________________________
54. ______________________________
55. ______________________________
56. ______________________________
57. ______________________________
58. ______________________________

59. ____
60. ____
61. ____
62. ____
63. ____
64. ____
65. ____
66. ____
67. ____
68. ____
69. ____
70. ____
71. ____
72. ____
73. ____
74. ____
75. ____
76. ____
77. ____
78. ____
79. ____
80. ____
81. ____
82. ____
83. ____
84. ____
85. ____
86. ____
87. ____
88. ____
89. ____
90. ____

91. ______________________________
92. ______________________________
93. ______________________________
94. ______________________________
95. ______________________________
96. ______________________________
97. ______________________________
98. ______________________________
99. ______________________________
100. ______________________________
101. ______________________________
102. ______________________________
103. ______________________________
104. ______________________________
105. ______________________________
106. ______________________________
107. ______________________________
108. ______________________________
109. ______________________________
110. ______________________________
111. ______________________________
112. ______________________________
113. ______________________________
114. ______________________________
115. ______________________________
116. ______________________________
117. ______________________________
118. ______________________________
119. ______________________________
120. ______________________________
121. ______________________________
122. ______________________________
123. ______________________________

124.____

125.____

126.____

127.____

128.____

129.____

130.____

131.____

132.____

133.____

134.____

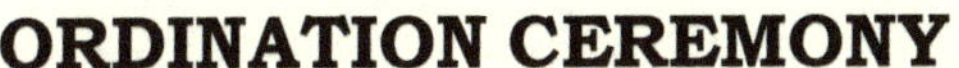

ORDINATION CEREMONY

THE IMPORTANCE OF ORDINATION

Throughout the history of Christianity, there has been the tradition of setting apart the official leadership of the church by a formal recognition process known as ordination.

The purpose of ordination is twofold: First, to signify that the individual has decided to devote his life to the mission of the church and second, to indicate that the church is approving and authorizing the individual(s) to serve the church in ministry. Ordination is a recognition of God's call and the church's approval.

It seems rather certain that the definite procedure of ordination began with the installation of the seven as assistants to the apostles in the Jerusalem church (Acts 6:6).

The several Greek words translated ordain in the New Testament mean "*to set apart to an office or special service.*" Three of those times it signifies formal induction into office (Titus 1:5; Hebrews 5:1; 8:3). And in one instance (Titus 1:5) it references a Christian office.

Where the word ordained is used for induction into office, it sheds no light on the details of procedure. They do not describe for us the ceremony of ordination. However, we can derive vivid and valuable suggestions from the record of the ordination of the seven in the Book of Acts, chapter 6:3-6. In these verses, the apostles assured the Jerusalem disciples that they would ordain the men selected to the task proposed. In verse 6, we are told they laid their hands on them.

The laying on of hands was a frequent and respected religious ceremony of the times, among both Jews and Christians. Thus, we have sufficient evidence that this was the most solemn and significant part of the ordination procedure in New Testament church (Acts 6:6; 13:3; 1 Timothy 4:14; 5:22; 2 Timothy 1:6).

The New Testament also furnishes grounds for the conclusion that ordination of ministers is more than an interest of the local church. Paul and Barnabas supervised the election of elders in the Galatian churches (Acts 14:23). Paul sent Titus to Crete to ordain elders in every city (Titus 1:5). And, we can infer that Paul and Silas supervised the ordination of Timothy (1 Timothy 4:14, 2 Timothy 1:6). Thus, we must conclude that while the elders were ordained for service in the local church, they were not ordained only as a function of the local church alone.

SELECTION OF NEW PASTOR

Ordination Council

The ordination council should be composed of the diocesan bishop, church board, ministers, and deacons that convene for the purpose of ordaining a minister to the lead a ministry. It should convene before the actual ordination service. The local church can create the ordination council by invitation or make use of a council provided by its association of churches.

Order of Business

The election of officers:

- a moderator to preside
- an examiner to question the candidate(s)

- a secretary to record the actions of the council

Questioning of the candidate—the moderator should ask the candidate to take a chair in front of the ordaining council, where he/she will be examined concerning his/her qualifications for the ministry. The questioning is led by the person elected to examine the candidate, and should last between 30 and 45 minutes.

Among the questions that should be asked are:

- Tell about your conversion experience
- Share what you believe about the Bible
- Narrate your understanding of God
- Tell how a person can be saved
- What is the New Testament church plan of salvation?
- What are the ordinances of the church and their significance?
- What is the mission of the church?
- Tell of someone you have led to faith in Christ
- Tell of your involvement in Christian ministry through the local church
- Who is the Holy Spirit?
- What is your belief about and practice of Christian stewardship?
- What do you believe about heaven?
- What do you believe about hell?
- What do you believe about the second coming of Christ?

- If this council should choose not to ordain you, what would you do?

The floor is then opened for questions from any member of the ordination council.

If the council is satisfied with the candidate's responses, a motion to recommend ordination to the church should be made and voted.

This action should be recorded by the secretary and a certificate of ordination signed by each member of the ordination council.

Pastoral Ordination Service

The purpose of an installation service is to establish a relationship between the new minister and the congregation. Either the Bishop of the Diocese or a designated officer shall perform the ceremony.

The officiating minister or master of ceremony shall provide the introduction.

Introduction

The office of the pastor has been instituted by Christ Himself as a gift to His Church (John 20:19–23; Ephesians 4:11–16). Through the Christian congregation, as the holder of all churchly authority, God calls qualified men and women to fill this divinely established office. Ordination is the solemn, public confirmation of that call (1 Timothy 4:14–16; Titus 1:5–9). The rites of ordination and installation are distinct. Ordination is the Church's recognition that a man has been rightly called by God through the Church into the office of pastor, whereas installation marks the beginning of a pastor's work in a particular place.

Prayer, Song, and Music

From the start, it is important to set a spiritual tone for the service which is accomplished well through a meaningful opening prayer. The prayer should mention the new pastor as well as offer praise to God for bringing a new leader to the church. The songs for the service should be uplifting, and, since this is a festive occasion, a soloist or special musical performance can be included as well.

The bishop or officiating minister shall deliver a sermon. After which, they shall speak the following or appropriate words:

> *Dearly beloved, the call of this congregation to Elder (Elder's name) to become pastor has been duly considered after inquiring into all circumstances. S/he has dignified her/his wellness to accept and we are here at this time by appointment and order of the (church organizational body or council) and by its authority; we now proceed to install (pastoral candidate's name) as the pastor of this congregation, in the name of the Lord Jesus Christ.*

Charge to the Pastor

The minister to be installed shall stand (with their spouse) before the officiating officer who shall propose the following questions:

Officiating minister

Are you willing to take charge of this congregation according to your declaration of accepting its call?

Answer

As God is my helper, I am willing.

Officiating minister

In taking upon you this charge, do you conscientiously believe and declare that you are influenced by a sincere desire to promote the glory of God and the good of the church?

Answer

As God is my helper, I so believe and declare.

Officiating minister

Do you solemnly promise that, with the assistance of the grace of God, you will live a holy and consecrated life while endeavoring faithfully to discharge all the duties of a pastor to the congregation? Will you be careful to maintain a moral standard in every respect as becoming a minister of the gospel of Christ and agreeable to your ordination agreement?

Answer

As God is my helper, I will.

The officiating officer shall propose the following question to the spouse:

Are you willing to be supportive of your husband/wife in their call to this ministry?

Answer

As God is my helper, I will.

Charge to the Congregation

Having received satisfactory answers to all these questions, the officiating minister shall propose to the congregation the following questions—requesting that they answer them in the affirming by holding up their right hand.

Officiating minister

Do you the people of this congregation continue to profess your readiness to receive Elder (Elder's name) whom you have called to be your pastor? With meekness and love, do you promise to receive the word of truth from his mouth and to submit to him in the due exercise of discipline? Do you promise to encourage him in his arduous work and to assist him in his endeavor for your instruction and spiritual education? Do you promise that while he is your pastor, you will assure his adequate maintenance by continuing to pay tithes and give offering and whatever else may be needed for the honor of religion and his comfort?

Congregation Answer

As God is our helper, we will.

After the people have answered the questions in the affirmative and while a suitable hymn is being sung, the deacons shall escort the new pastor to the pulpit where the officiating minister shall say the following words:

In the name of the Lord Jesus Christ, the great Head of the Church, and by the (church organization or council), I do pronounce and declare that Elder (pastor's name) is duly constituted the pastor of this congregation. Let us therefore pray unto God, the foundation of all grace and glory, that He may be pleased to sanctify with His heavenly blessing this relationship between pastor and people, which has now been established in His name. Amen.

Following the charge to the congregation:

- ❖ A prayer of blessing and dedication
- ❖ An appropriate hymn
- ❖ Remarks from the new pastor and spouse

Benediction

Hand of fellowship to minister and spouse.

A reception honoring the candidate and family.

The Ordination Of Deacons

If a pastor follows the right process, ordaining deacons can be a blessing to them and the church. What process should a pastor follow?

The Greek verb diakoneo from which the noun "deacon" comes meant "to serve." The word literally meant "through dust." Although the origin of the word is unknown, the concept of raising dust suggests a servant hastening to serve or wait on his master.

The deacon is a servant. He will do whatever needs to be done.

Preach two sermons and/or teach three bible surveys on the office of deacon using the classic scriptures found in Acts 6:1-6 and 1 Timothy 3:13-18. The minister may preach or teach on the spiritual requirements of a deacon; moral requirements of a deacon; the doctrinal requirements of a deacon; personal qualifications of a deacon; the ministry of a deacon; the marriage of a deacon.

Call the church to pray for wisdom and the leading of the Holy Spirit.

The deacon selection process should involve the pastor meeting individually with each candidate who is to be ordained, along with the candidate's spouse, having an understanding both will give full cooperation to serve the church.

Set the ordination service at a regular service, possibly an evening service.

Use no outside help! The pastor shall have charge of the service and it should be a dedication service for the entire church.

Let the church know the seriousness of the service. Let the church know they have a responsibility to these candidates.

At the close of the ordination service, have the candidates kneel in the congregation with their spouses standing back of them. Let the deacons and other ordained ministers lay hands on these men. Close with a prayer led by the pastor.

THE ORDINATION SERVICE

The ordination of deacons differs from that of a minister in several ways. First, more than one deacon is often ordained at the same time, while generally only one minister is ordained at a time. Also, other churches and ministers of the local association are usually involved in the ordination of a minister. But the ordination of a deacon is usually a local church event.

Order of the Service

The local pastor presides over the ordination service.

The questioning of the candidates, which should last between thirty and forty-five minutes, is led by the pastor. The questions may be alternated among the candidates:

Share your conversion experience.

What is the role and responsibility of a deacon?

What is the mission of the church?

What does the Bible teach about Christian stewardship?

Tell of some person you have led to Christ.

Present the plan of salvation. Share what you believe about the Bible.

If the pastor is satisfied with the examination, a motion to recommend ordination to the church is made and approved.

Hymn of dedication

Prayer

Testimony by each candidate

Recommendation of the ordination to the church to ordain

Special music

A message of challenge to the church and a charge to the deacons

The laying on of hands—The candidate kneels at the altar and ordained ministers and deacons walk by, lay their hands on his head, and offer a prayer.

Prayer of dedication

Presentation of ordination certificate signed by the pastor

Hand of fellowship is given to new deacons and their spouses by the church

A reception honoring the new deacons and their families

Deacons Duties In The Church

Deacon Ordination Charge

The highest honor a layperson can ever receive is to be elected a deacon by the church. However, no one should look upon the office as a position of honor only. One preacher said of his deacons, "We made an in-depth study of our deacons and discovered that half of them were too heavy for light work and half of them were too light for heavy work. So, none of them are working."

It's a sad day when the office of deacon becomes a place of honor instead of a place of service. The responsibility to execute one's duties in this office is perhaps as great as that of a minister when the matter is reduced to its basis.

Duties

What are the duties of deacons? In the Bible, the primary emphasis is given to what a deacon is to be, not what a deacon is to do. The inference is, if a person is what he ought to be, he will do what he ought to do.

- Be assistants to the pastor
- Be servants to the church
- Be an example of faithfulness to the world

Pastor's Assistant

- Assist in baptisms, communion, and foot washing services
- Accommodate and serve guest ministers in the absence of the pastor
- Provide and familiarize guest ministers with the procedures and methods of worship services
- Provide guest ministers with bulletins, songbooks, etc., for active participation in worship services

Board of Deacons

- Care for the poor, sick, and distressed
- Encourage peace, unity, and purity of the congregation

- Promote brotherhood, fellowship, and loyalty among members of the congregation
- Discover new areas in which saints may serve others
- Consider matters brought to the attention of the board and determine with the pastor if action is necessary—and if so, what action?

Hospitality

- The deacon board should always remember that they are appointed by the pastor and in authority only as long as that pastor is in office. If and when a new pastor comes into authority of that church, he/she can re-appoint or make new deacons and officers of the church if he/she so wishes.

Church Guide

- Select, train and maintain a staff of Church guides. Those guides should be available to conduct interested persons on tours of the church.

Flowers

- See that flowers for the sick and shut-ins are delivered to the persons suggested by the church office.
- Oversee floral tribute in special cases as directed by the board.

Evangelism

- Be alert to discover prospective new members.
- Advise the church office of emergencies requiring the attention of the pastor or other offices.
- Assign an active family in the church to each new member for one year. The assigned families should become friends of the new member, live nearby, be of the same age group, or have common interests.

Activities

Provide supervision for church events or arrangements:

- Father and son dinner
- Church picnic
- Thanksgiving service
- New Year's Eve dinner
- Special congregational events as directed by the pastor or church board
- Young people programs such as church services, recreation events, and etc.

Parking Lot Supervision

- Assume responsibility for the selection, training and maintenance of a staff. This will ensure proper handling of the parking at each regular church service and at special services as designated.

Purpose

The deacons' and ministers' wives are called with their husbands and should be honored in the church. This is a spiritual office and should be held with dignity and respect.

Commonly, the functional service of the deacons has been traced to Acts 6:1-7. The three main purposes of deacons are:

- First, deacons are to be assistants to the pastor.
- Second, deacons are to be servants to the congregation. What is the nature of the service of a deacon? The nature may vary from church to church and from time to time. However, it should include ministering to the sick; ministering to the bereaved; visiting the unsaved; visiting the unaffiliated; building the Christian fellowship; welcoming new members; performing acts of benevolence; administering the ordinances; promoting family worship.
- Third, deacons are to be examples of faithfulness in church and to the world. As a deacon, you were elected to solve problems, not create them.

As a result of this writing, may the pastor have an assistant, the congregation have a servant, and the world have an example of faithfulness.

CHURCH BUILDING PROJECT

Laying The Cornerstone Of A Church

Introduction

As a new building of worship is being constructed and a cornerstone, a specially designed and dated stone placed when two walls are joined at a corner, is ready to be set, a service commemorating the progress of the building shall be held. The cornerstone provides an inner chamber for placing a specially constructed box holding a variety of selected items. The service may follow a worship service, or may be held at a convenient time for as many as possible to join in the celebration.

Affirmation (officiating minister)

In ancient times, God commanded His servant Moses to set up the tabernacle in the wilderness camp of Israel. Later, He gave His blessing to King Solomon as he erected the Temple in Jerusalem, where all Israel worshiped. Now, He has moved your hearts to build this Holy Sanctuary for His worship and the assembling of His people for praise, prayer, and scriptural instruction. Today we gather in celebration looking toward the completion of this building of God as we ask God to grant us His blessings in this program.

Invocation (guest minister)

Holy God, we are here today to lay the cornerstone for this house of worship. We have come this far by faith and we do not doubt Your approval for our Godly purpose. We build this sacred place for worship, praise, prayer, and instruction in Your Word. We ask that you establish this Church upon the immovable and everlasting rock of faith, and that truth will be shared within our congregation, community, and the world. We pray for Your presence as we share our witness for Jesus Christ, our Lord, and Savior, in whose name we pray. Amen.

The people assembled shall rise, and the officiating minister shall say:

Our help is in the name of the Lord who made heaven and earth. Except the Lord build the house, they labor in vain that build it.

While the congregation is still standing, the minister will responsively read the following verses *(1 Chronicles 29:10-18).*

Officiating Minister

Blessed be thou, Lord God of Israel our father, forever and ever.

Congregation

Thine, O Lord is the greatness, and the power, and the glory, and the victory, and the majesty: for all that is in the heaven and in the earth is thine; thine is the Kingdom, O Lord, and thou art exalted as head above all.

Officiating Minister

Both riches and honor come of thee, and thou reignest over all; and in thine hand is power and might; and in thine hand it is to make great, and to give strength unto all.

Congregations

Now therefore, our God we thank thee, and praise thy glorious name.

Officiating Minister

But who am I, and what is my people, that we should be able to offer so willingly after this sort? For all things come of thee and of thine own have we given thee.

Congregation

For we are strangers before thee, and sojourners as were all our fathers, our days on the earth are as a shadow, and there is none abiding.

Officiating Minister

O Lord our God, all this store that we have prepared to build thee an house for thine holy name cometh of thine hand, and is all thine own.

Congregation

I know also, my God that thou triest the heart, and hast pleasure in uprightness. As for me, in the uprightness of mine heart I have willingly offered all these things; and now I have seen with joy thy people, which are present here, to offer willingly unto thee.

All Together

O Lord God of Abraham Isaac, and of Israel, our fathers, keep this forever in the imagination of the thoughts of the heart of thy people, and prepare their heart unto thee: Glory be to the Father and to his Son, and to the Holy Ghost. As it was in the beginning, is now; and ever be, world without end. Amen.

An appropriate hymn shall be rendered—after which the officiating minister shall say, repeat after me the following:

Direct us, O Lord, in all our doings with thy most gracious favor, and further us with continual help;

that in all our works begun, continued, and ended in thee, we may glorify thy holy name, and finally by thy mercy obtain everlasting life, through Jesus Christ our Lord. Amen.

Selected solo or choir songs may be rendered at this time.

The laying of the stone will follow the rendition.

Placing of the Contents

This could include, a brief history of the church, a picture of the church in progress, the church membership list, names of those contributing to a cornerstone offering, Pentecostal ministerial manual, a Bible, church bulletins of new church progress, newspaper accounts, or other memorabilia.

After such documents and other articles that are to be preserved have been deposited in the cavity prepared for them, the minister and other persons appointed for the purpose, assisted by the builder, shall lay the stone in its place. Then the officiating minister, placing his hand on it, shall say the following words:

Officiating Minister:

In the name of the Lord Jesus Christ, we lay this cornerstone of the house to be erected here under the name of ____ Church, and devoted to the worship of Almighty God. Behold, I lay in Zion, a Chief cornerstone, elect, and precious: and he that believeth in Him shall not be confounded. For other foundations can no man lay than that is laid, which is Jesus Christ. Amen.

Call to Respond

Minister shall say to the congregation—repeat the following:

Lord God, who are the beginning and the end, by whom all things were created, grant us the fullness of thy mercy and establish thou this stone which we plant in thy name. Accept, we beseech thee, the humble service of all who contribute their substance unto this building. Let blessings rest upon them and upon those who labor in erecting it; to shield them from all accidents and dangers. Grant unto them and all of us here present thy heavenly grace, that all our gifts and services may be sanctified, and, in soul and body, we may become living temples of the Holy Ghost. All which we ask through the abundant merits of our Lord and Savior who liveth and reigneth forever. Amen.

The Lord's Prayer Said in Concert

Our Father which art in heaven, Hallowed be thy name.

Thy kingdom come. Thy will be done in earth, as it is in Heaven.

Give us this day our daily bread.

And forgive us our debts, as we forgive our debtors.

And lead us not into temptation, but deliver us from evil: For thine is the kingdom, and the power, and the glory, forever. Amen.

The main address or sermon shall be delivered at this time. Afterward, an offertory for the building fund should be taken.

A selected solo or choir song may be rendered at this time.

Benediction.

Church Dedication

The entire program should leave a lasting impression of the sacredness of God's presence in His temple.

After being received by the deacons and trustees of the host church, all ministers shall be led into the sanctuary by the bishop of the diocese.

During the processional, the bishop or a designated minister shall read and appropriate scripture.

The assembled congregation shall stand. The *24th chapter of Psalms* will be read responsively either by the officiating minister or those who are taking part in the ceremony.

Prayer, Song, and Music

From the start, it is imperative to set a spiritual tone for the service which is accomplished well through a meaningful opening prayer. The prayer should mention the new pastor as well as offer praise to God for bringing a new leader to the church. The songs for the service should be uplifting, and, since this is a festive occasion, a soloist or special musical performance can be included as well.

Selected solo or choir song may be rendered at this time

Prayer is to be offered by the presiding minister or his designate

The congregation will stand while the presiding minister renders the Lord's prayer

Our Father which art in heaven, Hallowed be thy name.

Thy kingdom come. Thy will be done in earth, as it is in heaven.

Give us this day our daily bread.

And forgive us our debts, as we forgive our debtors.

And lead us not into temptation, but deliver us from evil: For thine is the kingdom, and the power, and the glory, forever. Amen.

The minister will speak the words of dedicatory while the congregation shall respond while remaining standing.

Officiating Minister

Almighty God, Father of our Lord Jesus Christ:

Congregation

To thee we dedicate this church.

Officiating Minister

The Lord Jesus Christ, who is the visible manifestation of the Father; immortal; blessed and holy Potentate; King of Kings and Lord of Lords; Prophet; and priest after the order of Melchizedek, in this name we have remission of sins and receive the gift of the Holy Ghost:

Congregation

To thee we dedicate this church.

Officiating Minister

Savior and God, giver of the Holy Ghost, head of the body, this is the church, sanctified, comforter and coming bridegroom:

Congregation

To thee we dedicate this church.

Officiating Minister

Arise, O Lord, into thy rest; thou and the ark of thy strength. Let thy priest be clothed with righteousness; and let thy saints shout for joy. Put thy name in this place; let thine eye be opened towards it and hearken unto the supplication of thy people when they pray in this place. In heaven, thy dwelling place, let thine hear, and when thou hearest, forgive. Amen.

The appointed minister shall offer a brief prayer of consecration

Selected hymnal or choir song may be rendered at this time

An offertory for the building fund is in order

The bishop of the diocese or designated minister shall deliver the sermon

At the Pastor's discretion, an altar call may be extended

Designated persons shall offer a brief prayer and benediction

Dedication Of Church Building Free Of Debt

Before any church building, parsonage, or other church unit is formally dedicated, all indebtedness against the same shall be discharged. The following service, commonly called a mortgage–burning service, may be used when the building has become free of debt and for the dedication of a church sanctuary, an education building, or activities building.

Gathering

Greeting

Officiating minister:

This is the day which the Lord has made; let us rejoice and be glad in it.

Congregation:

I was glad when they said to me, "Let us go to the house of the Lord!"

Officiating minister:

This is none other than the house of God, and this is the gate of heaven.

Congregation:

Blessed be the Lord; may God's glory fill the whole earth.

Hymn of Praise

If the hymn is a processional, it may precede the Greeting.

Opening Prayer

Eternal God, let this building, which we dedicate to your name, be a house of salvation and grace where souls gathered together may worship you in spirit and in truth. May we learn of you, and may grow together in love. Grant this through Christ our Lord. Amen.

Hymn or Other Act of Praise

Scripture (suggested)

1 Kings 8:22–30 (Solomon's prayer dedicating the Temple)

Isaiah 55:6–13 (God's Word shall not return empty)

Jeremiah 31:31–34 (The new covenant)

Psalm

Psalm 24

Scripture (suggested)

1 Corinthians 3:9 –13, 16–17 (Jesus Christ is the foundation).

Ephesians 2:13 –22 (Christ Jesus is the cornerstone).

Revelation 21 (The holy city)

Hymn or Song

Scriptural Reading (suggested)

Matthew 7:24 –27 (A house built on rock)

Matthew 16:13 –18 (On this rock I will build my Church)

Matthew 21:12 –17 (My house shall be a house of prayer)

Sermon

Burning of the Mortgage

The original mortgage should be preserved, but a copy ought to be burned.

Fire codes in some communities may require that the service or part of it be held outdoors. The service might begin in the church building and move outdoors in a procession for the mortgage burning. Such a procession is appropriate in any event, either at the beginning of the service or immediately before the burning ceremony. During the ceremony, the copy of the mortgage may be presented to the pastor or another ecclesiastical official by one of the trustees. The ceremony may include the bringing forward of the document to be burned in a vessel such as a large bowl. The burning may be accompanied by an anthem of praise or a brief witness to the congregation by several representatives of the different ministries of the church—worship, education, evangelism, or mission—concerning the meaning of this event and hopes for the future.

Offering

Act of Dedication

Any sections below that do not apply to the functions of the building being dedicated may be omitted.

Minister

Dear saints and friends, now that we have completed this building and paid all indebtedness on it, let us dedicate it and rejoice in its holy use.

To the glory of God, who has called us by grace;

to the honor of Jesus Christ, who loved us and gave himself for us;

to the praise of the Holy Spirit, who illumines and sanctifies us;

Congregational Response

We dedicate this house.

Minister

For the worship of God in prayer and praise;

for the preaching of the everlasting gospel;

Congregational Response

For the celebration of the Holy Sacraments;

Minister

For the comfort of all who mourn;

For strength to those who are tempted;

Congregational Response

For light to those who seek the way;

Minister

For the hallowing of family life;

For teaching and guiding the young;

Congregational Response

For the perfecting of the saints;

Minister

For the conversion of sinners;

For the promotion of righteousness;

Congregational Response

For the extension of God's reign;

Minister:

In the unity of the faith;

In the bond of brotherhood and sisterhood;

Congregational Response:

In love and goodwill to all;

Minister:

In gratitude for the labors of all who love and serve this church;

In loving remembrance of those who have finished their course;

Congregational Response:

And in the hope of eternal life through Jesus Christ our Lord. Amen.

Closing Prayer

We now, the people of this congregation, surrounded by a great cloud of witnesses,

grateful for our heritage, aware of the sacrifices of our mothers and fathers in the faith,

and confessing that apart from us, their work cannot be made perfect,

dedicate ourselves anew to the worship and service of Almighty God;

through Jesus Christ our Lord. Amen.

Hymn

Dismissal with Blessing

Baby Dedication

Baby Dedication Instructions

Introduction

It is exciting whenever a child enters a family. There is no greater moment than when parents sense that children are a gift from God. In these joyful moments, pastors have the privilege of sharing how parents can express their full appreciation to God through baby dedication.

Counseling for Baby Dedication

Dedicating a child acknowledges God's sovereignty not only over the child, but also the parents. The parents present their child before God and His people, asking for grace and wisdom in carrying out their responsibilities. Parents also come praying that their child might one day trust Jesus Christ as Savior for the forgiveness of sin.

Before the actual ceremony, it is crucial that pastors counsel parents about the meaning of dedication. The best passage for discussion is Deuteronomy 6:4-7. First, it commands parents to love God. If they truly wish for their child to one day love and follow God, their lives must be an example. This is a good time to query parents about their own personal relationship with Christ.

Second, Deuteronomy makes clear that the duty of teaching children belongs to parents: Sunday schools can provide weekly instruction, but parents must seize the teachable moments that arise throughout life. Explain the value of prayer at meal times and before bed. Urge them to read aloud Bible stories for devotions. Give them practical ideas they can implement into their daily family routines.

Sometimes it is custom for parents to choose godparent(s) for their child(ren). Often viewed merely as an honorary title, its value can be greatly enhanced by defining how this role will be carried out. Many godparents assume responsibility to provide cards and gifts of a Christian nature for the child on birthdays and holidays. Some periodically ask the parents how they are doing in training their child (Proverbs 22:6). Still, others have arranged that in the event of the parents' unexpected death, the godparents will take the child into their home (this, of course, requires legal documentation).

Conducting the Ceremony

On the day of the dedication, meet with the parents a few minutes before the service to explain where they should stand. For the services given below, the following advice is suggested: with the pastor standing front and center in the sanctuary, the father should stand immediately to the pastor's right, with the mother and any other children next to the father. Godparents and grandparents should stand to the pastor's left. Have the wife hold the baby as the family comes forward. During the service, the wife will pass the child to the father for the vow of dedication; the father holding the child during this time symbolizes that the husband is the family's spiritual head. Afterward, the father is then able to pass the baby to the pastor for the prayer of dedication.

Be sure to recognize everyone who stands before the church, especially siblings of the child being dedicated. Though this is not their special day, it is important to confirm that they too are key participants.

When grandparents stand, you may want to insert the following:

"Standing before us are three generations. Seeing this brings to mind Proverbs 17:6 which tells us that 'Grandchildren are a crown to the aged, and parents are the pride of children.'

(Name of grandparents), we know you are very proud of these grandchildren. And (name of parents), we trust that the step of faith you are taking today will make (Child's name) one day proud of your actions."

Finally, keep in mind that babies are unpredictable. Some may sleep during the dedication, but others might cry, especially while you are holding them! Humor is a delightful way to make light of the situation and dissipate any of your own uneasiness. It is moments such as these that make baby dedications so memorable. The sacred and the mundane collide. And through it, we see a glimpse of the glorious gospel- God being found in the appearance of man.

Baby Dedication

Sample 1

Preparation for Baby Dedication

It is my distinct privilege and honor today to perform the dedication of these children. I have never made it a secret how strongly I feel about the dedication of babies and I feel that strongly *today. You hold in your arms the blessings of the Lord upon your life. Scripture says...*

Lo, children are an heritage of the LORD: and the fruit of the womb is his reward. As arrows are in the hand of a mighty man; so are children of the youth. Happy is the man that hath his quiver full of them: they shall not be ashamed, but they shall speak with the enemies in the gate (Psalms 127:3-5).

The Bible is simply saying that children are an inheritance from the Lord and will become a reward to the righteous. According to the Bible children are like arrows - a type of strength - to their parents. Children have a way of strengthening your maturity, they strengthen your level of responsibility and sometimes strengthen your trust in God.

This/these child(ren) has/have and will continue to have an indelible impact on your life. By the very same token, your life and how you live will also have an eternal impact on their life.

Scripture says:

The just man walketh in his integrity: his children are blessed after him (Proverbs 20:7).

As surely as your home will be blessed by the presence of these children they will be blessed or cursed by the life you live in front of them. This is one of the reasons we have baby dedications; to put these children in God's hands and to put our minds into the proper perspective of our responsibility.

Service of Dedication

In this service of dedication, we:

1. Give thanks to God for the creation and birth of this/these child(ren).
2. Make a solemn promise as parents and as a Church that we will join our efforts to provide guidance for these children in instruction, in discipline, and in experiencing God's plan of salvation.
3. Pray for God's blessings upon these children and offer them, in due time, back into the service of the Lord.

Both Parents

And now I acknowledge (parent's names) who present this/these child(ren) before God and this congregation that God called His Church. Would you please state the full name(s) of the child(ren) you now hold and present for dedication? (Await the response)

I now ask your close attention and your honest response to each question posed.

The Father

Do you (father's name), as the father of (baby's name) by your own free will, desire to offer this child to the Lord? (Await answer)

Do you vow to be the head of your family, serving as a Priest, provider, and protector? (Await answer)

Do you vow to love and take care of this mother, in every way, and to bring this/these child(ren) up in the fear and admonition of the Lord? (Await answer)

The Mother

Do you (mother's name), as the Mother of (baby's name) by your own free will, desire to offer this/these child(ren) to the Lord? (Await answer)

Do you vow to be a Christian wife to your husband, taking care of his every need, and be a help in raising this/these child(ren)? (Await answer)

Do you vow to be a God-fearing Mother to these children, bringing them up in the nurture and admonition of the Lord? (Await answer)

Both Parents

Do you both promise to uphold God's command He said?

Hear, O Israel: The LORD our God is one LORD: And thou shalt love the LORD thy God with all thine heart, and with all thy soul, and with all thy might. And these words, which I command thee this day, shall be in thine heart: And thou shalt teach them diligently unto thy children, and shalt talk of them when thou sittest in thine house, and when thou walkest by the way, and when thou liest down, and when thou risest up (Deuteronomy 6:4-7 KJV).

Is it your intention to minister this precious Apostolic truth to this/these child(ren)?

The Congregation

Do you, as the congregation of (Church's name), promise to join these parents in the teaching and training of these children? And do you promise to minister to them in the Apostolic doctrine with Apostolic methods until they come to know God themselves in the power of the new birth experience? If you accept this responsibility would you please indicate it by standing? (Await response)

Prayer

Take baby(ies) in your arms if possible

[Any additional remarks]

Having accepted this responsibility and acknowledged these vows, I count it a privilege to dedicate this/these child(ren) to the Lord.

Dedicatory Prayer

Baby Dedication

Sample 2

Children are a gift from God. Psalm 127:3 proclaims that "Sons are a heritage from the Lord, children a reward from Him." As believers, we are called to recognize that children belong first and foremost to God. God, in his goodness, gives children as gifts to parents. They not only have the great responsibility of caring for the gift, but also the wonderful privilege of enjoying the gift. Because children belong to God and are given by grace as gifts to parents, it is only proper and appropriate that children be dedicated back to God.

We are told in 1 Samuel 1 that Hannah presented her son Samuel to the Lord. In Luke 2:22 we read that Mary and Joseph brought their baby Jesus to the temple in Jerusalem to present him before the Lord. In the same way, (parent's names) bring their (son/daughter and child's name), presenting first themselves and then their (son/daughter) before the Lord our God.

Accompanying them in making this commitment are (child's name) godparents, (Godparent's name). And witnessing this as well are (parent's other children).

(Parents), God's instructions are plain, and I call your attention to the commands recorded in Holy Scripture. Deuteronomy 6:4-7 tells us:

"Hear O Israel: The Lord our God is one. Love the Lord your God with all your heart, and with all your soul, and with all your strength. These commandments that I give you today are to be upon your hearts. Impress them on their children. Talk about them when you sit at home and when you walk along the road, when you lie down and when you get up."

Ephesians 6:4 says:

"fathers, do not provoke your children to wrath; instead, bring them up in the training and instruction of the Lord."

(Parent's names), love God with every ounce and fiber of your energy and teach (child's name) to do the same. As you love God, one another, and (other children's name(s)), you will model before (child's name) a wonderful love for God that he/she will want for himself/herself.

(Parent's names), by coming forward before God and his people, do you hereby declare your desire to dedicate yourselves and your (son/daughter and child's name) to the Lord? If so, please respond by saying "we do." ("We do.")

Having come freely, I ask now that you enter into the following commitment in the presence of God and his people (wife hands child to husband as a sign of his spiritual headship in the family). So that (child's name) may walk in the abundant life that Christ offers, do you, (parent's names), vow that by God's help and in partnership with the church, to provide (child's name) a Christian home of love and peace, to raise him/her in the truth of our Lord's instruction and discipline, and to encourage him/her to one day trust Jesus Christ as his Savior and Lord? ("We do.")

Modeling this kind of love cannot be done alone. It requires the help of others. For this reason, (parent's names) call upon the help of (godparent's names). I now direct my questions to you. By coming forward before God and his people, do you hereby declare your desire to help (parent's names) fulfill the vow they have just made by becoming (child's name) godparents? If so, please respond by saying "we do." ("We do.")

Having come freely, I ask now that you enter into the following commitment: so that (child's name) may walk in the abundant life that Christ offers, do you vow, by God's help, to encourage (parent's names) through praise and correction in their effort to raise (child's name) in the fear of the Lord, to uphold them in prayer, and if anything should happen to (parent's names), to assume responsibility in helping (child's name) receive our Lord's guidance and instruction? ("We do.")

Finally, I ask that the church make a vow as well. There's an old proverb that says, "it takes a village to raise a child." Parents have first responsibility, but they also need the help and support of the community. So, I direct my questions now to the church. By being present in God's house today, do you hereby declare yourselves to be the children of God because you trust in Jesus Christ alone for the forgiveness of sins and the gift of eternal life? If this is true, please respond by saying "we do." ("We do.")

Would you please stand? Having come freely, I ask now that you make the following commitment to those who stand before you: so that (child's name) may walk in the abundant life that Christ offers, do you vow, by God's help, to be faithful in your calling as members of the body of Christ, to help (parent's names) be faithful to God, and to help teach and train (child's name) in the ways of the Lord so that he/she might one day trust Him as Savior and Lord? If you accept this responsibility, please respond by saying "we do."

(Dad hands child to pastor for the prayer of dedication)

(Presentation of Certificate and Gift)

(May wish to sing dedication hymn)

www.ingramcontent.com/pod-product-compliance
Lightning Source LLC
LaVergne TN
LVHW090953080826
845145LV00003B/995

* 9 7 8 1 7 3 2 0 5 8 6 9 9 *